THE GREAT NORTHERN RAILWAY IN THE EAST MIDLANDS

The Erewash Valley Lines
Pinxton Branch, Awsworth - Ilkeston
Heanor & Stanton Branches

ALFRED HENSHAW

THE RAILWAY CORRESPONDENCE AND TRAVEL SOCIETY
2000

©RCTS 2000

ISBN 090 1115 886

121 Green End Road, Sawtry, Huntingdon PE28 5XA.

Front Cover Captions

Top Left
A good view of Pinxton station from the embankment of the colliery branch line showing LNER class L1 Tank 67741 having arrived with a train from Nottingham Victoria. The original corbels on the Station House chimneys have been removed, and the Goods Yard sidings are full of wagons being stored prior to breaking up. Away to the right is a northbound empties train on the Midland Railway lines.

April 1962, J Cupit

Middle
The Giltbrook Viaduct seen from beside the Nottingham Canal facing southeast. Concrete girders replace the original swingbridge. The signal post on the embankment left of the viaduct holds the up distant for Awsworth Junction above which was Digby Sidings starter before the signalbox was burnt down. The Greasley arm of the canal branched left through the wide arch right of the bridge handrails to Digby Colliery on the north side of the viaduct.

August 1965, A Henshaw

Bottom Left
LNER class L1 2-6-4 Tank 67769 enters Eastwood station with the 6.56 pm passenger train from Pinxton to Nottingham Victoria. The pump house chimney, water crane and North signal box are seen more clearly here.

June 1959, W R Sheppard

Top Right
A typical mixed goods train with Class B headlamps struggling up the steep incline caused by subsidence at bridge 48, behind an Ivatt class J6 0-6-0. The rather grandiose station nameboard reads: 'Kimberley for Watnall, Nuthall and Giltbrook' 'Change for Pinxton and Derby Trains'.

c. 1950, H H Mather

Bottom Right
This early picture of Ilkeston station, looking east, is taken from the Up platform, and shows clearly the main buildings and Stationmaster's House on the opposite side, and conforming to the standard pattern. The additional building nearer the bridge would be for porters and other staff such as shunters, one of whom can be seen with his shunting pole on the right, for the room between the urinals and Ladies waiting room was used as the stationmaster's office. The lattice girder footbridge connecting the platforms was later boxed in when extensions were made. The Heanor road crosses by bridge 62, immediately behind this footbridge.
Note the angled nameboards on each platform, an unusual feature, beneath which is a notice 'Change for Marlpool and Heanor'. Beyond the nameboard on the left is a cast iron urinal which was removed in 1940, with those at Awsworth and Kimberley, to assist the war effort.

c.1910, Author's Collection

Back Cover Captions

Top
This wide angle view of the south side of the Ilkeston (Bennerley) Viaduct as seen from beside the Erewash Canal gives an impression of curvature at the east end but it is actually straight. The change to brick pillars and wrought iron girders over the MR Erewash Valley lines is on the left, with part of the opencast coal blending plant behind the slender girders of the viaduct. The MR lines are seen on the right with a signal post. The tall building on the left beneath the branches of the tree is the rapid loading bunker.

May 1987, A Henshaw

Middle
A sadly forlorn view of Heanor station with no regular passenger service, showing BR Standard Class 2MT 2-6-2T 41320 with RCTS Special. The lines no longer extend beyond the bridge. To the left is the goods shed and dock. The NCB 0-6-0 saddle-tank engine can be seen near the screening plant (right) for loading opencast coal from the area.

September 1959, John Marshall

Bottom
Having climbed for three miles up the bank from Basford through Watnall tunnel, a W.D. austerity 2-8-0 still has steam to spare on the next two miles downhill to the Erewash Valley at Bennerley. Its mixed goods train from Colwick to Stanton is mostly of ironstone passing through Kimberley station seen from the signalbox this affords a good view of the up side waiting rooms and footbridge which earlier was clad with corrugated iron sheeting obscuring the view of the station.

June 1965, A Henshaw

Title Page Captions

A view showing LNER Ivatt class J6 64202 with a Grantham-Derby passenger train in Kimberley station. The lattice work of the footbridge was backed by corrugated galvanised sheets along its whole length.

March 1957, H. H. MAther

Printed by Birlim Litho Limited
230 Cinderhill Road, Bulwell, Nottingham, NG6 8SB.

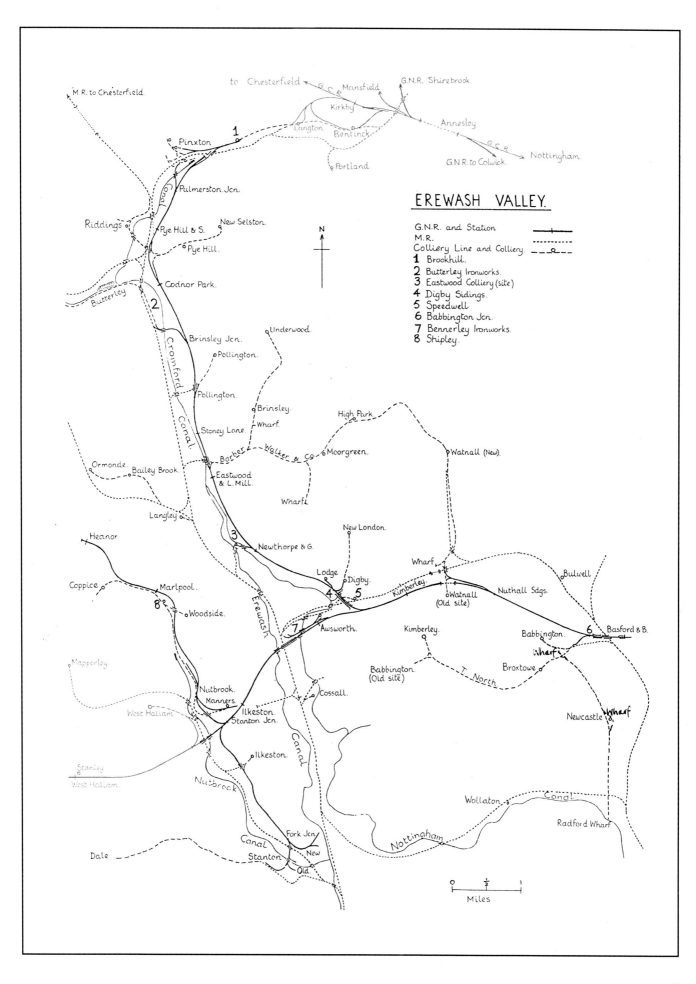

EREWASH VALLEY.

G.N.R. and Station	
M.R.	
Colliery Line and Colliery.	

1 Brookhill.
2 Butterley Ironworks.
3 Eastwood Colliery (site)
4 Digby Sidings.
5 Speedwell
6 Babbington Jcn.
7 Bennerley Ironworks.
8 Shipley.

N

KEY TO DIAGRAM ABBREVIATIONS AND SYMBOLS

BH - Booking Hall.

BO - Booking Office.

CB - Clearance Locking Bar.

CLC - Cheshire Lines Committee.

FB - Foot Bridge.

FP - Foot Path.

GCR - Great Central Railway.

GNR - Great Northern Railway.

LC - Level Crossing.

LDECR - Lancashire, Derbyshire
& East Coast Railway.

LR - Lamp Room.

MP - Mile Post.

MR - Midland Railway.

PLH - Platelayer's Hut.

SB - Signal Box.

SM - Station Master.

SP - Signal Post.

TC - Track Circuit.

TT - Turntable.

WB - Weighbridge.

WR - Waiting Room.

MPD - Motive Power Department

LMR - London Midland Region (BR)

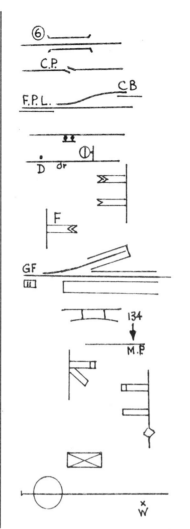

Bridge & Numberplate.

Catch Points.

Clearance locking bar.
Facing Point Lock.

Detonator Placers.

Disc or Ground Signal.

Distant Signal worked from Signalbox illustrated.

Distant Signal NOT worked from Signalbox illustrated.

Distant Signal Fixed at Caution.

Dock (loading).

Platform.

Ground Frame.

Loading Gauge.

Mile Post.

Signal Slotted with next signalbox.

Stop Signal worked from signalbox illustrated.

Stop Signal NOT worked from signalbox illustrated.

Track Circuit Indicator.

Signalbox

Turntable and Water Column.

METRICATION

The units of measure used in this book are taken from the original drawings and documents. In many instances these are British Imperial units, the conversion to metric being shown below:-

1in			=	2.54 centimetres
1ft	=	12in	=	30.48 centimetres
1yd	=	36in	=	0.9144 metres
1 chain	=	22yds	=	20.1168 metres
1 mile	=	1,760yds	=	1.6093 kilometres

DECIMALISATION

Decimal Currency was introduced in the UK in the 1970s. The old £sd currency has been used in this book for historical accuracy. One new penny (1p) is equal to 2.4 old pence (2.4d). Note that the handbill and ticket illustrations use the alternative presentation of currency values, e.g. fares of 2 / 6 (or 2s 6d) equates to 12½p.

CONTENTS -
THE EREWASH VALLEY LINES
PINXTON BRANCH, AWSWORTH - ILKESTON
HEANOR & STANTON BRANCHES

GRADIENT PROFILES

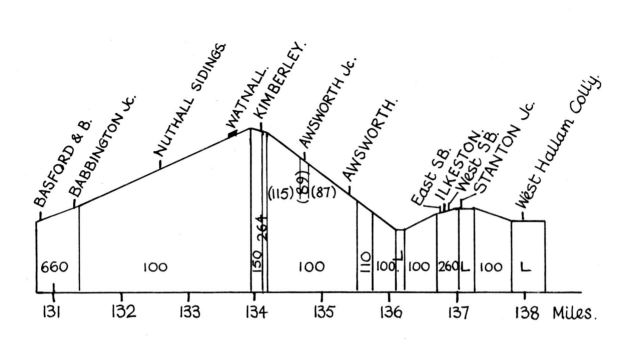

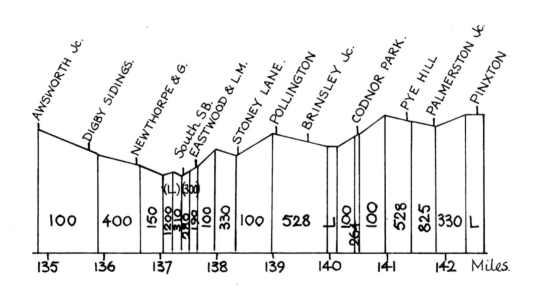

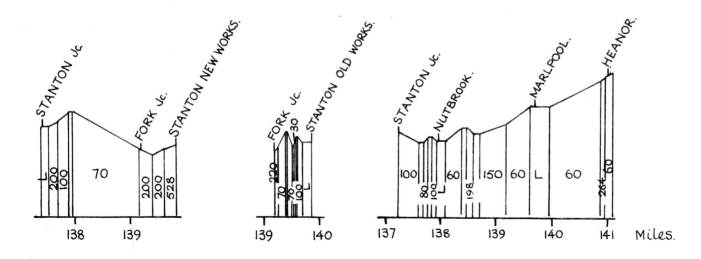

AUTHOR'S NOTE

The scale plans of layouts for the lines west and north oc Colwick yards thereof are taken from GNR drawings dated 1903 and 1904 by kind permission of BR Public Relations Officer and the Engineer's Department. In the few cases where these were unavailable use has been made of OS 1:1250 scale maps, First or Second Editions.

The Signalbox diagrams are not to scale. They show details of lever frame connections to points, signals, etc, and other relevant information, and are taken from the author's (including H H Mather's) collections and date from 1935 to 1970. They should make a useful comparison with the scale maps, revealing closure of early collieries/works together with the opening of such new sites as Opencast coal sidings in the Second World War.

Distances shown on the scale plans are from the GNR Appendix to the Working Time Table of June 1912 and agree with the re-measurement of the lines from King's Cross Passenger Station undertaken during 1895-6. Mile posts on early OS maps do not necessarily coincide with official mileages.

Gradient profiles have been taken from LNER charts of the 1930s, and particularly in colliery regions, where subsidence has occurred differ from original GNR drawings made at the opening of the lines. Earlier figures are shown in brackets.

Apart from early Post Cards, and Bridge photographs from BR archives, many illustrations are of the post-war era. Every effort has been made to include early pictures, and the date together with the photographer is always mentioned where known. The age of many of the photographs has affected their quality of reproduction.

The lines covered have been walked and photographed recently to indicate what remains to be seen of a once busy railway.

ACKNOWLEDGMENTS

Having been left the task of writing the text for the third section of the GNR in the Nottingham District due to the sad demise of Harold H Mather in 1985, I must thank his son, David H Mather, for his co-operation and assistance in providing his father's notes, and many documents which he has inherited relating to the area. My thanks also extend to the following:-

British Rail Engineers and Publicity staff at Nottingham; J Cupit and staff of the Nottinghamshire County Records Office; Staff of Derbyshire Records and Museums Offices; C H Eggleston, J W D Miller, F Pike, P Stevenson, W Taylor, M J Hitchens, M Back, S Checkley and G H R Gwatkin. For the generous use of photographs and drawings, all of which are acknowledged in the text where known, my thanks include John R Bonser, I Cook, D Corns, A G Cramp, M P D Hammond, M Higginson, C A Hill, John Marshall, W Nelson, E Parker, H J Priestley, R W Sheppard, B Walker and J P Wilson. To Birlim Litho Ltd, I am indebted for great guidance and assistance in the layout of text, illustrations and captions much needed by an inexperienced late comer to producing these books.

Much assistance has come from reminiscences with friends too numerous to list in the Railway Correspondence and Travel Society, the Railway and Canal Historical Society and ex-colleagues from L&NER days. They will know to whom I refer and forgive me for omitting their names, I trust.

NOTES ABOUT THE AUTHORS

Work on this history of the former London and North Eastern Railway in the East Midlands first started after two former colleagues, Alfred Henshaw and Harold Mather, began reminiscing about their careers and the fact that there was no complete record of the lines they had once worked on.

Harold had been involved with the local railways all his life. His grandfather was engaged in the construction of the GNR Derbyshire Extension and when this was completed was stationed at Breadsall as foreman ganger until his retirement in 1915. Harold's father started work with the GNR as a locomotive cleaner in 1898 at Nottingham London Road Locomotive Depot, then as Fireman at Derby before transferring to Colwick in 1915 and retired from the Nottingham District Control Office in 1947. Harold joined the LNER in 1924, spending all his railway career in Derbyshire, Leicestershire, Northamptonshire and Nottinghamshire. After working through the clerical grades and as relief clerk working at many stations in the East Midlands he became Station Master in 1944. For twenty years his stations featured in the Best Kept Station and Gardens Competitions, winning many First Prizes. He became Area Manager in 1965 and finally retired with the closure of Colwick and the Derbyshire Extension Lines in 1970. Harold Mather also had a wide interest in the preservation of our heritage and was the author of the History of Kimberley and the History of the Clock and Watch Makers of Nottinghamshire. Sadly Harold became seriously ill in 1985 and died before the work on the four volumes could be completed, leaving Alf to finish the work.

Alfred joined the LNER in 1934 and served as goods and booking clerk at several stations in the Nottingham area until 1938 when he transferred to the Nottingham District Control Office. Apart from his army service he spent the rest of his railway career working on the three control sections which were responsible for the operation of services over the lines covered by this history. Alf left the railway service at Nationalisation in 1948 to train as a school teacher. However, his keen interest in the railway industry continued and over many years he has lectured on the local railway history.

After many months of hard work completing his diagrams, maps and photographs, Alf has rewritten the early manuscript using Harold's original detailed notes and documents which have been generously made available together with much helpful advice by his son, David H Mather.

John Marshall is a well established railway historian, author of several books and articles for the railway press. Upon learning of the efforts of Alf Henshaw to complete the books on the GNR in the Nottingham area, after the death of Harold Mather, John offered to use his wealth of material and knowledge of the area to write an introductory historical chapter for each volume.

1. HISTORICAL INTRODUCTION - BY JOHN MARSHALL

THE GNR EXTENDS INTO DERBYSHIRE
by John Marshall

While the MR was presenting its London Extension Bill the GNR, frustrated in its attempt to secure a fair share of the Derbyshire coal traffic, decided on 28 October 1862 to survey a line from Nottingham to the Derbyshire coalfield. Richard Johnson (1827-1924), Chief Engineer of the GNR, carried out the survey and a Bill was presented for a line from Colwick, round the north of Nottingham to Kimberley and up the Erewash Valley to Codnor Park in the heart of MR territory, at an estimated cost of £350,000 (*Railway Times* 14 February 1863 p 178). The original Ambergate line would have crossed the Erewash near Codnor Park. Although coal traffic had passed from the MR over the Grantham line since 1852, it was mostly local traffic because the Midland would not make reasonable rates to London for coal by this route. It was hoped that the new GNR Bill would force the MR to modify its rates, and indeed it did (*Railway Times* 15 August 1863 p 1104). A 'Coal Traffic Agreement' was signed, on 23 January 1863, under which the GNR reduced its rates for MR coal trains between Hitchin and London in exchange for access to the Erewash Valley over the MR for the same rates. The GNR thereupon withdrew its Codnor Park Bill before the Committee stage, but the MR would not withdraw the Bill for its London

extension which was built, and was opened on 13 July 1868.

Once its independence was established the MR, on 24 March 1871, lowered its coal rates from Derbyshire to London and withdrew the through rates for GNR trains. Then, having expelled the GNR, the MR increased its rates for Derbyshire coal. At the same time the GNR management was engaged in a dispute with Edward Watkin, of the Manchester, Sheffield & Lincolnshire Railway, over through rates for South Yorkshire coal. The outcome was a revival of the GNR Codnor Park Bill of 1863 in a revised form, presented for the 1872 session, for an extension from two junctions with the Nottingham-Grantham line at Colwick, round the north of Nottingham to Awsworth beyond Kimberley. From here one branch would go up the Erewash valley to Pinxton and the other through Ilkeston and Derby to join the North Staffordshire Railway near Egginton.The Bill passed through Parliament and received the Royal Assent on 25 June 1872 (GNR [Derbyshire & Staffordshire] Act 1872 c139, 25 June).

The Act authorised construction of 39 1/2 miles of railway: from two junctions near Colwick to Kimberley and Pinxton; from near Kimberley to a junction with the North Staffordshire Railway near Egginton; a connection from here to the NSR Burton branch, and various other short connections. Section 19 imposed a penalty of £50 per day if the railway was not opened in five years from the passing of the Act. Power was given to raise £1,000,000 by new

Fig. 1
This is the GNR official photograph of bridge 37 facing north from the junction of the MR Bennerley branch left and the Leen Valley lines at Basford Junction. Of particular interest is the footbridge which connects a public footpath between the enbankments either side which is supported over the rails by brackets from the main girders. The oak fencing on the right is clearly seen descending the embankment. Note the tall bracket signals with early markings on the rear sides of these semophore arms.

c. 1910, Courtesy British Rail

Fig. 2
A general view of Babbington Colliery yard facing west, which includes the headstocks and screens on the left, and the engine shed with a diesel shunter in the doorway, together with an 0-6-0 saddle tank of standard design used widely by the NCB in this area.

July 1957, John R Bonser

shares, to borrow £333,000 and to create and issue debenture stock. No time was lost and on 16 August 1872 the order was given for 'the railway from Nottingham to Pinxton to be proceeded with as rapidly as possible'.

The work was carried out under Richard Johnson and the resident engineer William Henry Stubbs (1847-90) who was later to become Chief Civil Engineer of the MS&LR. Contract No 1, Colwick to the east end of Ilkeston viaduct was let to George Benton and Abraham Woodiwiss for £298,744 on 4th March 1873. Heavy engineering was required in cuttings, tunnels, embankments and viaducts.

Beyond Basford station, 9 1/4 miles from Colwick, the line crossed the Nottingham - Mansfield branch of the MR at a height of 40 ft by an iron lattice deck span. A viaduct of nine brick arches carried it about 50 ft above the River Leen. A short branch here served Cinderhill and other collieries of the Babbington Coal Company. Two miles further

was Kimberley cutting, 55 ft deep and 2 1/2 miles long, through magnesian limestone which proved exceedingly difficult to excavate because of trouble with water, and Watnall tunnel, 268 yds, caused so much delay that to get the line opened throughout, a temporary single track was laid on gradients of 1 in 30 over the top (there is a photograph of this on p305 of Grinling's *History of the GNR* 1903, 1966). The eastern part of this temporary line remained in use afterwards as a connection to Barber Walker's Watnall colliery lines. The cutting extended to Kimberley station, beyond which the main turnpike road was lowered to pass beneath the line. Later, to allow the electric trams of the Nottinghamshire & Derbyshire Tramway Co to pass under the bridge, the road was lowered still further. The trams began operation between Nottingham and Ripley on 1 January 1913. At Awsworth Junction the Pinxton branch turned off to the right, and the portion of the line in Contract No 1 ended at the east end of the Ilkeston viaduct.

Fig. 3
The west portal of Watnall tunnel built and lined with the magnesian limestone from the cutting. Note the stone steps and handrail over the entrance leading to the top of the cutting on the left, giving access for telegraph linesmen to the telegraph poles which were along the top of the cutting. On the right are catch points with a 'Switch' sign. The eastern portal differed in coming to a point above the entrance.

c.1904, Courtesy British Rail

Fig. 4
The steps to the subway and Station Road on the western side of bridge 47, across the Main Street, Kimberley. The lower stories of the old Great Northern Hotel are on the left. Note the bracket for a gas lamp on the stone retaining wall above the steps. These steps and the area around the crossing gates were ideal for childrens games of chasing, or hide and seek to the annoyance of the signalman or porter on duty.

May 1966, A Henshaw

Contract No 2 comprising Railways 3, 5 and 6 in the Act totalled about 8 1/2 miles from Awsworth Junction to a junction with the MR at Pinxton. On 22 August 1873 the tender of Joseph Firbank for £161,500 was accepted. A short distance north of Awsworth Junction was Giltbrook viaduct, the largest engineering structure on the line. The red brick viaduct of 43 spans formed a reverse curve and was 1716 ft long and had a maximum height of 60 ft. It was in four sections: the first with one span of 27 ft and 13 of 30 ft; second with one skew arch of 27 ft over the MR Bulwell - Bennerley branch (built in opposition to, and closely paralleling the GNR line and completed in 1879), and 15 of 30 ft; third with one 27 ft skew arch, in the opposite direction, over a mineral railway to Digby colliery, and three of 30 ft; fourth a 45 ft segmental arch over an arm of the Nottingham Canal and eight spans of 30 ft. The sections were separated by massive stop piers. Two arches contained houses. From the north end of the viaduct another colliery branch dropped down on the right to the Digby colliery system.

Fig. 5
The NE side of Giltbrook Viaduct, seen from above Awsworth Lane, which passed beneath the first arch. Uncluttered by shrubs or trees, the Midland Railway embankment is seen clearly, and beyond are the Digby Colliery sidings. On the left is the cast iron trespass warning and the Down branch starting signal post (later moved to a position over the Midland lines). Behind the third telegraph post is the chimney of the Nottingham Gas Light and Coke Co's chemical works.

c.1905, British Rail

Fig. 6
The SW face of the viaduct as seen from the main lines beyond Awsworth Junction., showing the later position of signal 6 (Fig.88 p40) without the distant arm beneath. (Notice the access arch (no 44) beneath the MR embankment and the upper two storeys of the dwellings built into the arch (no 13) above the asbestos roof (centre)). The chemical works stood between the embankment and the Greasley Arm of the Nottingham Canal.

July 1966, A Henshaw

The line passed through Newthorpe station 15 1/4 miles, and Eastwood & Langley Mill, 16 1/4 miles. North of here connection was made with the colliery railway system of Barber Walker & Co for which extensive sidings were provided. Few heavy earthworks were needed to carry the line up the east side of the Erewash valley. A mile and a half north of Eastwood a connection was made on the right with the branch from Stoneyford Junction on the MR to New Brinsley (Pollington) colliery. At Brinsley Junction a branch turned off left to Codnor Park Ironworks, and at Jacksdale was a brick viaduct of 20 spans on which a station, at 19 1/4 miles, was built. Originally this was named Codnor Park & Selston for Ironville and Jacksdale. It was renamed Codnor Park on 22 May 1901 and Jacksdale on 1 July 1950. Further sidings were provided for the Oakes company's collieries and ironworks. Next was Pye Hill station, 20 miles. Just beyond here a branch turned off

left, bridged the Alfreton - Selston road and joined the MR at Canal Junction. It is shown as a through connection on the 1880 1:2500 O.S. map. The date of closure was probably after the Brinsley connection was opened in 1899. A new station, Pye Hill & Somercotes, was opened further north, closer to the road, on 8 January 1906.

A cutting 60 ft deep carried the line through Pye Hill; half a mile beyond this another branch crossed the Erewash to serve the Pinxton collieries. The line terminated 3/4 mile beyond here at Pinxton for South Normanton station, 21 1/2 miles. All the station buildings were erected by Kirk & Barry of Sleaford whose tender of £37,252 was accepted on 6 November 1874. Ironwork, amounting to about 1400 tons, was supplied and erected by Pitts & Co of Stanningley, Leeds.

Fig. 7
With the Up Main line in the foreground, this view from the embankment just south of the viaduct 11 shows the sweep of the full or loaded wagon sidings from Moorgreen Colliery and the Barber Walker network of pits beyond, to the GNR at Eastwood North. The line of wagons, extreme left, passes beneath the south spans of the viaduct to the empties sidings (Fig.128 p56). In the background is the growing spoil heap from Moorgreen Colliery, now rounded on top and landscaped by the NCB, covered in grass.
The foreground and sidings area was opencast mined for coal prior to the extension of the A 610 by-pass from Langley Mill to Codnor in 1983.
November 1955, John R Bonser

Fig. 8
A good panoramic view of the viaduct on which Codnor Park station was built seen from the remains of the Portland Canal Wharf at Jacksdale. The tramway to this wharf from the Selston pits passed beneath the skew arch on the right, and the public road giving access to the station carrying the platform and Down side building show clearly from the semicircular arches carrying the track, as do the brick pillars supporting the platform and subway from the timber supports of the extension to the canal arch. The end of the Goods shed and office appear on the left-hand edge of the picture.
April 1956, P Stevenson

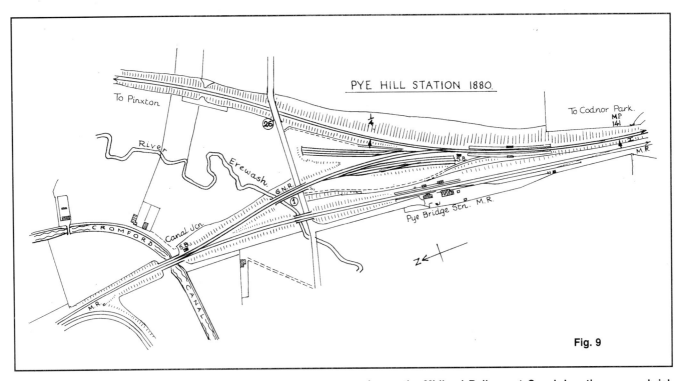

Fig. 9

This map shows the layout at the time of opening with the connection to the Midland Railway at Canal Junction over a brick viaduct 1 of six spans which was destroyed by coal subsidence after a few years. To maintain running powers over Midland Railway for their Manchester traffic, the GNR extended the Brinsley branch to cross the Cromford Canal and join the Midland Rly at Codnor Park GN Junction, which opened in 1899 at around the same time as the Deansgate Goods depot in Manchester.

Goods and coal traffic began on Monday 23 August 1875. The section from Colwick to 'New Basford' as it was originally named was opened for passenger traffic on 1 February 1876 with seven trains each way, weekdays only, taking 22 minutes from Nottingham. On 26 February 1876 it was reported that the passenger service to New Basford had not yet built up, but the Pinxton line was carrying a considerable tonnage of coal. New Basford station was renamed Basford & Bulwell at the opening for passengers to Pinxton on 1 August 1876. (It became Basford North on 21 September 1953.) There were nine trains each way daily between Nottingham and Pinxton taking an hour. Two extra ran on Saturdays and there were three on Sundays. By August 1878 the daily service had been reduced to six each way taking about 55 minutes.

An outcome of the GCR London extension through Nottingham Victoria was the building, at enormous expense, of the Deansgate goods warehouse in Manchester, authorised by the 1895 Act mentioned earlier (GNR Act 1895 c36, 30 May). This was partly opened on 1 July 1898. By way of opening up a route from Nottingham the GNR built a connection from the Codnor Park Ironworks branch at Brinsley Junction to the MR Erewash Valley line. This was opened on 1 November 1899. A nightly freight service was operated between Colwick and Manchester in both directions. With the opening of this connection the earlier one to Canal Junction at Pye Hill was abandoned, and the viaduct was later demolished. A new station was opened at Pye Hill, north of the original station and nearer to the main road. The GNR had running powers over the

Fig. 10
A close-up of the 1905 bridge 33 seen from the Midland Railway, facing west, with a Down train approaching Sleights East Signal box.
c.1906, Courtesy British Rail

MR to New Mills *via* Chesterfield and the Hope Valley and, until 1914, *via* Ambergate also. Mileage from Colwick was 77, about 17 miles less than the GN/GC route *via* Shirebrook, Sheffield and Guide Bridge. Through traffic ran until 1953. The warehouse was closed on 29 March 1954 and the junction at Brinsley was taken out on 4 July 1954.

At Pinxton a short branch was built to new collieries beyond the station. It began south of the station, crossed over the MR, to serve Brookhill, Bentinck and Langton collieries. The tender of Hemingway & Co, £3567, was accepted on 25 March 1904. The branch was passed by the Board of Trade inspector on 13 October 1905.

With the Pinxton line almost completed, on 6 June 1875 the contract for the section from Awsworth Junction to Derby was awarded to Benton & Woodiwiss for £242,500. The line was laid out by Richard Johnson, and the resident engineer was Samuel Abbott. From Awsworth Junction the line descended at 1 in 100 through Awsworth station, 14 1/4 miles, opened 1 November 1880, to the principal

engineering work, the viaduct across the Erewash valley near Ilkeston. The ground here was not firm enough to support a brick structure, so an iron viaduct was erected, 1452 ft long. The 16 lattice deck spans, 76 ft 7 in, stood on piers each consisting of 12 wrought iron columns on foundations of blue bricks capped by stone. The foundations were begun in May 1876 and the girders were erected, from the west end, between July 1876 and November 1877. The rails were 60 ft 10 in above the bed of the Erewash. Three additional iron skew spans of 35 ft 4 1/2 in, 52 ft 1 in and 26 ft 0 in on brick piers carried the railway over the Erewash valley line of the MR. Ironwork was supplied by Eastwood, Swingler & Co of Derby (*The Engineer* Vol 44, 19 October 1877, pp 274-7). Ilkeston station, 15 3/4 miles, was sited just west of the main road to Heanor.

Since 1795 coal from the Shipley colliery in the Nutbrook valley north-west of Ilkeston had been passing down the Nutbrook Canal. Under its Act of 1866 the MR built a branch from Stanton Gate up into the Nutbrook valley taking a large share of the traffic. The GNR crossed this branch

Fig. 11
The Ilkeston (Bennerley) viaduct, south side, facing NW towards Cotmanhay. Between the first and second columns from the right can be seen the offices of the Bennerley Ironworks Company, though the site was being worked for opencast coal. At the far left the brick columns and abutments carry a bridge over the Midland Railway Erewash Valley lines.
May 1974, John Marshall

Fig. 12
A general view of Heanor station and yard, showing left to right, Stationmaster's house, dilapidated platform buildings beside the arrival road, and goods shed beyond the heaps of coal.
1963, D H Mather

just west of its bridge over the Nutbrook Canal. Eager for a share of the Shipley colliery traffic the GNR obtained powers in its Act of 1880 (GNR Act 1880 c140, 6 August) for a branch of just under a mile from Ilkeston to the Nutbrook colliery of Shipley Collieries. Before any work was carried out on this, further powers were obtained in the 1885 Act (GNR [Various Powers] Act 1885 c76, 16 July) for a branch of over 3 miles from a junction with its Main line at Ilkeston to Shipley and a short connection to Nutbrook colliery. Major Marindin sanctioned its opening for coal traffic from Nutbrook colliery on 4 June 1886.

By a further Act in 1887 (GNR Act 1887 c93, 5 July) powers were obtained for an extension of the Shipley branch to Heanor and for alteration of the levels on the branch. On 1 November 1889 the tender of J Tomlinson, £22,007, was accepted for construction of the Heanor branch. Passenger traffic began on 1 July 1891 with seven trains to Heanor and six return daily and one extra on Saturdays, taking ten minutes from Ilkeston. To accommodate the branch passenger train an additional platform was built on the up side of Ilkeston station. The branch was single-track beyond Nutbrook Sidings and there was one intermediate

station, at Marlpool, 2 3/4 miles. Heanor station, 4 1/4 miles, consisted of an island platform beyond which the tracks extended under the Derby road to end in a blind cutting. A scheme to extend the branch to Alfreton was never carried out. Goods traffic to Heanor began on 1 January 1892.

To the south of Ilkeston were Ilkeston Colliery, and ironworks at Stanton and Hallam Fields. In its Act of 1882 (GNR Act 1882 c191, 10 August) the GNR obtained powers for a branch of just over 2 1/2 miles from Stanton Junction, Ilkeston, to Stanton works; also a connection to the railway from Ilkeston Colliery to the Nutbrook branch of the MR and a connection to the sidings of Hallam Fields Ironworks of the Stanton Iron Co. On 6 October 1882 the tender of Henry Lovatt, £30,262 was accepted for construction of the branch and connections. According to Wrottesley (Wrottesley, J, *The Great Northern Railway* Vol 2, p144, Batsford 1979 ISBN 0 7134 1592 4) coal traffic from Ilkeston Colliery began on 9 July 1883 and was worked by the Contractor's engines. The Stanton Ironworks branch opened on 3 September 1883 and the Hallam Fields connection early in 1884.

Fig. 13
Facing the opposite way from bridge 9 is bridge 15, which can be seen in the distance beyond which the branch terminated. On the right are the School buildings, evacuated and not used after 1940 because of danger from enemy action during the war. The string of high-sided coke wagons appears ready for despatch.
January 1968, A Henshaw

2. BABBINGTON JUNCTION - AWSWORTH JUNCTION

BABBINGTON JUNCTION 131 m 24 1/2 ch

Opened August 1875 with a branch to serve Cinderhill Colliery, which joined an existing single line branch from the MR at Basford Junction to the colliery, at Cinderhill Junction, a Midland Railway signal box. This box was closed in the 1950s under BR LM Region operations, after which all the coal was taken *via* the Midland route. Since 1984, the Midland branch has been lifted, any coal from the colliery being raised at Hucknall No.2.

Thomas North (1811-1868) was an important mining entrepreneur whose early shallow mines in the first half of the 19th century were sunk in the Babbington, Strelley, Cossall area. He constructed standard gauge railway lines from his pits there, to both the Nottingham and Erewash canals at Cossall.

In 1843 he sank new shafts at Cinderhill, installing up-to-date equipment, connecting the older workings at Babbington, now almost worked out, with a railway which needed rope haulage up the slope to the high ground at Swingate (Kimberley). Pits were sunk at Swingate in 1855, and Broxtowe in 1863, the line connecting these forming a triangular junction with that from Babbington village (see Map, frontispiece). A TV mast stands at this site now, forming a prominent landmark. For transporting the coal from these newer collieries, Thomas North built a line parallel with the Nottingham turnpike road (now A 610), beside which a pit called Newcastle was sunk in 1853. The line turned south to reach a wharf on the Nottingham Canal at Radford. There were Landsale Wharves at Cinderhill and Newcastle. His railway bridged the Nottingham-Ripley road at Cinderhill (Fig.31 p15) and to connect to the Midland Rly at Basford, North built bridges over the road to Bulwell, and Bagnall

Road, and extended his railway as far as their Leen Valley Line. A few years later the Midland Railway purchased this line and built the signal box at Cinderhill Junction to allow the GNR access to the colliery traffic from Babbington Junction. After North's death, the collieries traded under the name 'Babbington', and their wagons carried this inscription in bold letters (Fig.26 p14).

The GNR signal box, perched on a high embankment above the Leen Valley, was worked by one Porter Signalman from Basford, who opened it for his 'Pilot', due from Leen Valley Junction with empties at 11.28 am, and closed after necessary trips to Bulwell Common had been made, and the booked departure for Colwick at 4.40 pm. One of the shunters at the colliery sidings ensured the GN side had plenty of the traffic by not always separating wagons routed *via* the Midland lines. 'Jock' knew that Colwick would be able to deal with all the traffic that was sent there!

However, by 1957 the pits at Newcastle, Broxtowe and Kimberley had been closed, and all traffic from Cinderhill was sent *via* the Midland route. The GN sidings were used for wagon storage as required until closure in September 1962, when the branch was lifted. It was demolished shortly afterwards, the derelict site being on offer for development. The track from Midland branch to the colliery was lifted also, and a Light Rapid Tramway System for passengers is planned to use the trackbed as a branch from the main system from the city to Hucknall and Mansfield, and to the Phoenix Park development at the colliery site.

Bridges 37, 38 and 39 have all been demolished, and the high embankments between removed. Bridges 2 and 3 on the colliery branch are still intact.

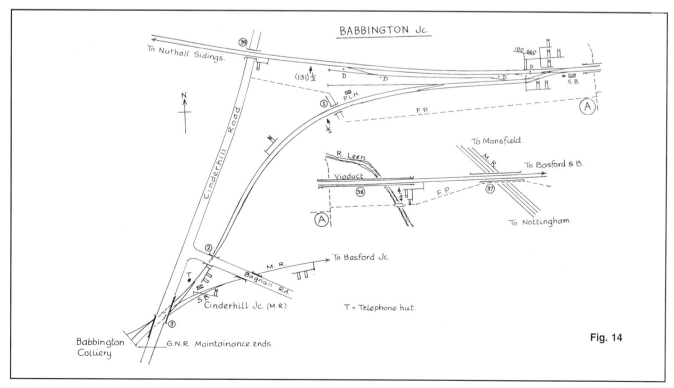

Fig. 14

Fig. 15
Bridge 2 beneath Bagnall Road seen from Cinderhill Junction. Old MR semaphores protect the junction painted with black circles on the back. The signal through the bridge is Babbington Junction branch distant, fixed at caution.
c.1904, Courtesy British Rail

Fig. 16
Bridge 3 under Cinderhill-Bulwell road seen from beside Cinderhill Junction signal box. The lines in the foreground are from Basford Junction MR, those to the right are the GNR lines to Babbington Junction. Note the circle on the arm of the Midland Railway Distant signal.
c.1904, Courtesy British Rail

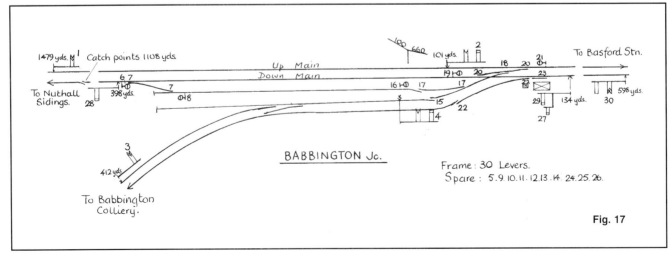

BABBINGTON Jc.

Frame: 30 Levers.
Spare: 5.9.10.11.12.13.14.24.25.26.

Fig. 17

Fig. 18
A view from beside the MR lines at Basford Junction showing a former LNER class J6 64215 on a local Derby passenger train passing westwards over bridge 37. The 9-arch brick viaduct spanning the River Leen is beyond the bracket signal, and the signal box is beyond the viaduct. Brackets which supported a wooden footbridge over the Midland line were still in place, as was the fencing down the slope of the embankment near the viaduct.
May 1955, J Cupit

Fig. 19
An aerial view of Cinderhill and Babbington Colliery facing north, showing the GNR line running from left to right across the top, with bridge 39 spanning the Cinderhill Road near the centre of the picture. Babbington Junction is just out of view, but a few wagons can be seen beside the main line and the sweep of the colliery branch into the sidings shows up clearly. Left of these sidings are the brick kilns and chimneys, and climbing southwards beside the quadrilateral of colliery cottages known as Holden Square is Thomas North's mineral line to Broxtowe and Kimberley pits. The old turnpike road into Nottingham, now the A 610, widened to a dual carriageway, runs diagonally from the bottom left corner, and the old Landsale Wharf was right of the mineral line (Fig. 21 p12).
c.1928, Courtesy Nuthall Local History Soc

Fig. 20
Here is a fine example of a GNR lattice girder bracket signal post with different sized somersault arms mounted on wooden posts. The larger arm (29) is the Down Home; the smaller one is for entry to the colliery branch. A Derby Friargate to Skegness train is coasting downhill past the signalbox, unfortunately directly behind the signal post, hauled by LNER Class K2 2-6-0 61773. Between the two telegraph poles on the left is the embankment of the branch as it falls to the colliery lines at Cinderhill Junction. The factory chimney right of the locomotive is at a dye works east of the Cinderhill Road.
Sept 1959, D B Swale

Fig. 21
This is the site of Thomas North's Landsale Wharf at Cinderhill, originally alongside the turnpike road which became the A 610, and which was spanned by bridge 5 on the extreme right. The colliery engine *Michael* is pushing a loaded train from the colliery sidings towards Broxtowe, to return along the curve on the left to the wharves at Newcastle and Whitemoor. Behind the train is the headgear above the shafts; the tandem gear partly obscured by steam was the first to be erected when the shafts were sunk. The building behind the bridge is the 'Colliers Arms' public house, now demolished. Note the water pipe and sock in the foreground.
Michael, six-coupled saddle tank, was built by Robert Stephenson & Hawthorn (Newcastle) in 1945, works number 7285. She was sent to NCB BA Collieries at Cinderhill on 1st January 1947. Rebuilt by Bagnall at Stafford in November 1956, she was returned to Clifton Colliery in November of that year: disposal unknown.
April 1955, John R Bonser

Fig. 22
This shows T North's line from Kimberley to Radford crossing Bell's Lane (Bulwell-Stapleford road). Bridge 5 can be seen left of the brick hut, and the pit headstocks are on the extreme left above the garage door. During the early 1930s Nottingham City built large estates of council houses at Aspley and Bilborough, and this road together with Broxtowe Lane were widened. This accounts for the pair of gates on either side which met in the middle of the road when rail traffic passed.
February 1967, A Henshaw

Fig. 23
This view, facing east from the Cinderhill Road bridge 3, shows Cinderhill Junction signal box. The tracks to the right lead to Basford Junction beneath Thomas North's bridge carrying Bagnall Road. To the left the track to Babbington Junction beneath bridge 2 has been lifted, but the Midland-type signals are clearly seen.
September 1963, P Stevenson

Fig. 24
Careful positioning of the photographer ensured a wealth of detail in this photograph which could easily have been missed. You are looking along the colliery branch, facing northeast from close beside the GNR Up fixed distant post, with the Midland Railway's distant from Cinderhill Junction beside the vacant line.
An LNER class K2 2-6-0 is hauling a good rake of loaded wagons with a spare brake in the middle, up the steep gradient to the sidings at Babbington Junction, which signal box can be seen above the roof

of the building beyond the gate. Over the train is the embankment carrying the main lines to Nuthall Sidings, with the Up Home signal 2 right of the disused Suncole plant, which was built in the late 1930s by Simon-Carves for a German firm, and which fell into disuse during the war. This plant was served by sidings from the Midland Railway's branch from Basford Junction. To the right of the signal box is the nine-arch viaduct spanning the River Leen and its flood plain (Fig.18 p11)
July 1957, John R Bonser

Fig. 25
Another scene in Babbington Colliery showing the saddle tank shunter at work. Named *Philip* this engine was built by Hunslet in 1943, works number 2854. It worked at Babbington Colliery from 1947 until 1964 when it was transferred to Clifton Colliery.
July 1957, John R Bonser

Fig. 26
Bridge 3 seen from the colliery yard. The colliery line to Broxtowe and Kimberley pits climbed away to the right behind the wagons. The notice board reads: 'No NCB engines to pass this point on any line without the permission of the shunter'.

May 1968, A Henshaw

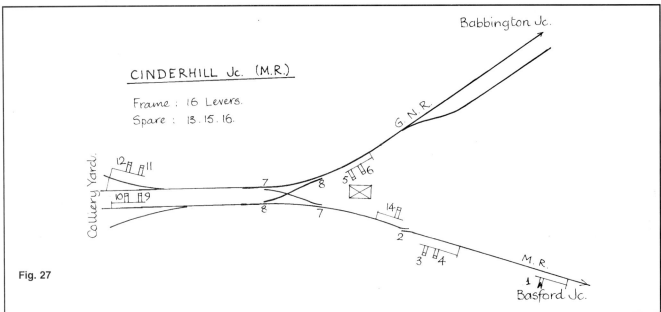

CINDERHILL Jc. (M.R.)

Frame : 16 Levers.
Spare : 13.15.16.

Babbington Jc.

G.N.R.

Colliery Yard.

M.R.

Basford Jc.

Fig. 27

Fig. 28
The GNR approach to Cinderhill Junction beneath bridge 2 carrying Bagnall Road over the branch, with the signal 'off' for entry to the colliery yard.

July 1957, John R Bonser

Fig. 29
Restored Private Owner's coal wagon seen at Loughborough Main Line Steam Trust.

May 1982, A Henshaw

Fig. 30
Babbington Colliery loco *Colonel* in the yard; a much earlier engine than the NCB standard saddle tank.

March 1953, John R Bonser

Fig. 31
T North's bridge 5 at Cinderhill immediately before demolition for widening the A 610 Ripley road to dual carriageway. The Colliery buildings and headstocks are in the background.
The small isolated building to the right of the colliery was the office where the miners received their weekly wage packets.
The mineral line now forms a road into Broxtowe Country Park, around the site of the old colliery.
The whole of the Cinderhill colliery site in the picture has been cleared, and a huge heap of spoil 'landscaped' and covered in grass extends westwards as far as Hempshill Vale new housing estate, close to the site of the sand siding (Fig.34 p16). The Phoenix Park development of hotels, light industries and Park-and-Ride facilities now occupies the pit yard.

May 1968, A Henshaw

Fig. 32
A view looking east through Hempshill Fan bridge 41. The branch into the Sand Siding trails into the Down main from the right where the front of the Ground Frame hut is just visible. The Fan was a ventilation shaft for Cinderhill (Babbington) Colliery situated to the right of the bridge. The engine house was gutted by fire about 1930, and not replaced.

c.1904,
Courtesy British Rail

Fig. 33
A Down passenger train climbing the bank at the overbridge 41 against the Ground Frame controlling the entrance to the first sand quarry. This was worked by the Stanton Ironworks Company which was behind the left hand embankment. The somersault signals are Sand Siding Down home and Nuthall Sidings Down distant. In 1929, the Stanton Co began working the land on the up side with a mechanical digger. A 3ft gauge line carried tippler wagons seen on the right, which were hauled across a girder bridge over the main lines by rope from a winch.

August 1959, John Marshall

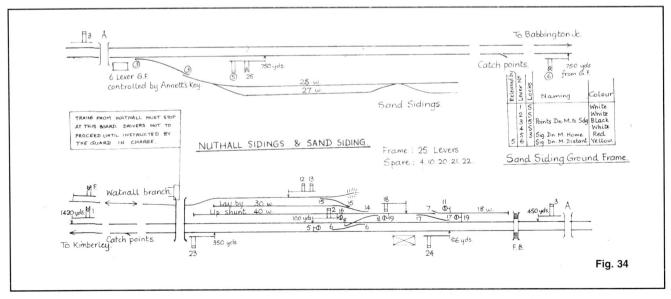

Fig. 34

NUTHALL SIDINGS & SAND SIDING.

TRAINS FROM WATNALL MUST STOP AT THIS BOARD. DRIVERS NOT TO PROCEED UNTIL INSTRUCTED BY THE GUARD IN CHARGE.

6 Lever G.F. controlled by Annett's Key.

To Babbington Jc.

Catch points.

Sand Sidings.

Frame : 25 Levers
Spare : 4.10.20.21.22.

Released by Lever Nº	Locks	Naming	Colour
1	S		White
2	S		White
3	S	Points Dn. M. to Sdg	Black
4	S		White
5	S	Sig. Dn. M. Home	Red
5	6	Sig. Dn. M. Distant	Yellow

Sand Siding Ground Frame.

Watnall branch.

Lay by   30 w.
Up shunt   40 w.

To Kimberley.   Catch points.

NUTHALL SIDINGS 132m 49 3/4 ch

This signal box, approximately half way up the 1 in 100 'bank' from Babbington Junction to Kimberley opened in August 1875 to deal with the first coal trains from the Pinxton collieries to Colwick. These trains came across the Alfreton Road (B600) at Watnall and down a steep gradient of 1 in 40 to join the Main lines at Nuthall Sidings because the contractors had not completed work through Watnall tunnel. However, the line east of the Alfreton road was connected to Barber-Walker's colliery lines from Watnall Old Colliery, which closed after their New Watnall colliery opened in 1875. It then formed the Watnall Branch. At the signal box two sidings were provided, one forming an Up shunt, together with a head shunt which needed an embankment and a retaining wall, built of local stone, to maintain its level against the falling gradient of the running lines (Fig.38 p18)

During the 1930s, severe colliery subsidence occurred here, necessitating permanent way speed checks of 20 mph, and each weekend ballast trains would come from Colwick to tip tons of ashes for packing the track. Although the track was packed, the signal box itself slowly settled until the outside platform for cleaning the windows was little above the track level. The point rodding from beneath was cranked up to track level; a most unusual sight! Eventually, after settlement, the original signal box was dismantled and replaced by a wooden one brought from Quainton Road (Metropolitan and GC Joint).

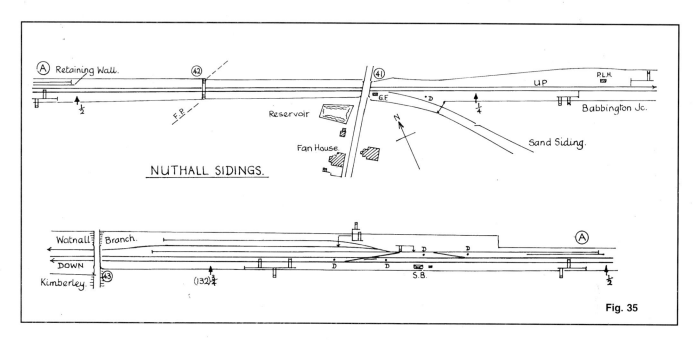

NUTHALL SIDINGS.

Fig. 35

Fig. 36
Bridge 43 facing east towards Nuthall Sidings. The Watnall branch climbs through the separate arch on the left. The signal post beside the Up main carries a repeating arm above for the Up home signal, also the Down starter signal which points to the right.
c.1904,
Courtesy British Rail

17

The first part of the cutting eastwards from the Leen Valley was through New Red Sandstone which overlays marl and the harder magnesian limestone found further along. The Stanton Ironworks Company exploited this, by starting a quarry on the south side of the GNR lines about 1898. This quarry was served by sidings worked from a Ground Frame of 6 levers in a hut beside bridge 41 at 132 m 25 ch, and called the Sand Sidings. It provided good quality moulding sand for the Stanton pig beds. In 1929 quarrying began on the north side of the Main lines, the sand being loaded into tippler trucks on a 3 ft gauge tramway. This crossed the Main lines on a light steel girder bridge so that the trucks could be loaded into the standard gauge wagons at the existing sidings. The tipplers were taken to the bridge by steam locomotive, but were drawn over it by rope, electrically driven. The quarries closed about 1960.

Fig. 37
This signal box, brought from Quainton Road (Met & GC) in the late 1930s, replaced the earlier one which sank some 8 ft due to colliery subsidence, which caused speed restrictions of 20 mph whilst engineers packed and filled in with ashes most weekends. Note the short bracket for the signal arm and lamp.

P Smith

Fig. 38
This view (facing east) from the signal box shows the earlier GN arm on the Down home signal. An LNER Class J39 with the breakdown train has arrived to re-rail two wagons at the end of the shunt spur. The 1 in 100 gradient is clearly visible beside this spur which is level.

1954/5, H H Mather

Fig. 39
Another view of the breakdown train at Nuthall Sidings, facing west along the Watnall Colliery branch (right) which climbs steeply beyond the single arch to sidings at 'The Top'.
1954/5, H H Mather

Fig. 40
Beyond the GNR maintenance point at Watnall 'Top' Barber-Walker's private line continued across the MR Basford-Bennerley branch over a slender iron girder and wooden bridge, just east of Watnall station.

As will be seen from the map of the Lower Erewash Valley (Frontispiece) it connected Watnall New Colliery to their existing network of collieries in the Brinsley, Moorgreen and Eastwood area. Branches also led to Landsale Wharves at Watnall, Newthorpe Dovecote Rd and Brinsley. This photograph taken from the top of the Midland cutting shows the bridge with buildings erected by the War Department in 1940 which were used by RAF Fighter Command operations. Note the use of limestone from the cutting for the pillars.

May 1956, A Henshaw

Fig. 41
This box camera view of the empties sidings at 'Watnall Top' is seen from the rear of a house near the NE end of Albert Avenue. Beyond the sheds and poultry houses is the oak fence boundary above the cutting containing the main lines, the opposite side of which has concrete posts and a wire fence. The colliery empties, nearly all lettered B&W Co, stand in the long siding on an embankment, to maintain level ground beside the branch which climbs at 1 in 40 past Redfield House to the right.

Pre-1940, Author's Collection

Fig. 42
Site of Watnall Colliery sidings at 'The Top'. The empties sidings were situated on the bank to the left which, being level, again indicated the steep gradient of the branch which ran from the roadway immediately past the right of the glasshouse. The screens for opencast coal, erected in 1941 are seen on the right.

July 1981, A Henshaw

19

THE WATNALL BRANCH

The single line branch to Watnall Top where it connected with Barber-Walker's lines from Watnall New Colliery was worked by Annett's Key from Nuthall Sidings. It crossed New Farm Lane on the level close to Bridge 44 where a gate house was built for the Crossing Keeper. During the 1930s the ganger Frank Lord lived here and his wife acted as Crossing Keeper. There was a flight of steps beside the bridge to reach the track below. Before reaching the Empties sidings another occupation road crossed to Redfield House at Bridge 45. Further along, the Empties sidings, lifted on a small embankment at the buffers to maintain level ground were passed on the left before reaching a STOP board near the shunter's cabin. Here a triangle was formed with the early colliery line from Watnall Old Pit, allowing Colliery engines to turn. GNR locomotives had to ascend the branch chimney first and return without turning because of the steep gradient. The left hand curve ended in buffer stops before reaching the Alfreton Road, which it had previously crossed to reach the Old Colliery, the site of which is a large mound overgrown with trees forming a play area in the Larkfields Housing estate. The right hand curve split into four sidings, used for the loaded wagons of coal and goods before joining the colliery line at a STOP board forbidding GNR engines from proceeding any further. This was because the colliery line crossed the Midland Railway's Bennerley Junction to Basford line by a girder bridge with a low wooden parapet

rail, quite flimsy in appearance (Fig.40 p19) before reaching Common Lane and the junction to Watnall Wharf (Landsale) at the B 600 Alfreton Road.

In 1941 the Ministry of Fuel and Power erected a screening plant and engine shed with additional sidings to deal with opencast coal from the area. These sidings were laid on the north side of the branch and included three beyond the gate house between the branch and the edge of the cutting. All were worked from connections to the branch by a second Annett's Key, kept at the top so that shunting could take place independently from the signalman's control at Nuthall Sidings. This increased the steady flow of traffic considerably during and immediately after the war years. Watnall New Colliery was closed in 1958 resulting in the closure of the branch. The opencast screens were not removed until the early 1980s, and the site is still used as a solid fuel storage and distribution area by the Fernwood Group.

In the mid-1960s the M1 motorway was built through Nottinghamshire,, opening as far as junction 28 at South Normanton, near Pinxton, whilst the work proceeded further north. This involved bridging the GNR lines over the cutting between bridges 43 and 44. The contractors were able to use the Watnall branch trackbed from New Farm Lane for plant and access to the site.

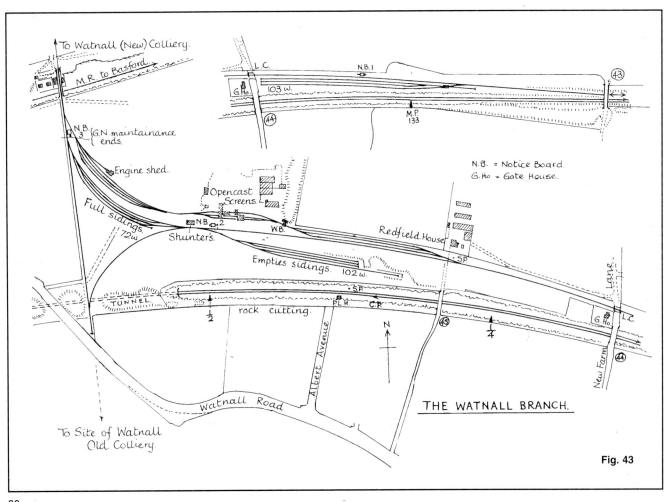

THE WATNALL BRANCH.

Fig. 43

In 1981-2 a new Outer Loop Road, named Low Wood Road, was built from the A 610 roundabout at Hempshill to join Hucknall Road at Bulwell. This crossed the GNR trackbed east of Nuthall Sidings between bridges 42 and 41 near the Sand Sidings site. Here, the cutting was filled in, the bridges demolished, and a large housing estate on the east side of this road stretches from Hempshill to Bulwell. The trackbed west of this development remains overgrown with young trees and shrubs, with a meandering stream flowing down the gradient from New Farm lane where bridge 44 has been filled in, together with the rest of the deepening cutting and Watnall tunnel itself.

In October 1995 a new housing development called Windsor Chase was built east of the B 600 and south of the infilled cutting and tunnel as far as the nursery near Albert Avenue and the site of bridge 45 (Fig.46 p22).

Fig. 44
Ex-LNER class J77 8416 at the opencast plant, Watnall. Extra sidings and a small loco shed were built on the north side of the branch to accommodate extra traffic during 1941. This engine was built at Gateshead in November 1877 as 0-4-4 Tank 71. Rebuilt at York as 0-6-0 in September 1901, sold to the Ministry of Fuel & Power, Broomhill 1950, and after repairs in 1951-2 came to the NCB at Watnall in 1954. It then worked in North Wales and was scrapped in about 1961.

1955, C A Hill

Fig. 45
This view, looking along the line of the Watnall branch towards Nuthall Sidings, shows the rear of the gatehouse, now renovated and having a garage, beside which can be seen one of the crossing gates at New Farm Lane.
When the parapet of the stone bridge 45 collapsed on to the track below in March 1955, BR repaired it with concrete planks and eventually demolished it in December 1970, thus severing the original access to Redfield House, which was replaced by use of the trackbed from the crossing.

July 1981, A Henshaw

Fig. 46
A view looking east of bridge 45, occupation to Redfield House beside the Watnall branch. Built of local stone, the arch springs from the rock of the cutting, as does the original bridge 44 seen beyond, which carries New Farm Lane over the main lines.

c.1904, Courtesy British Rail

Fig. 47
The same bridge seen from the top of the cutting showing concrete repair work to the parapet which collapsed in March 1955, necessitating closure of the lines for 24 hours. After this event, vehicular access to Redfield House was *via* New Farm Lane and along the bed of the Watnall branch, whose rails had been lifted. The bridge was demolished in December 1970 and the cutting, together with Watnall tunnel, filled in with waste between bridges 44 at New Farm Lane and 46 at Kimberley.

October 1967, A Henshaw

Fig. 48
The M1 bridge almost completed. A Stanier Class 8F with a train of mineral empties for Colwick is about to pass beneath. Large drain pipes were laid beneath the tracks beyond the bridge where the fencing is seen. Note 133 mile post bottom centre.

September 1967, A Henshaw

Fig. 49
An extra bridge was built across the lines between bridges 43 and 44 in 1965 as the M1 motorway was extended northwards. The Watnall branch trackbed to the right provided ready access for contractor's plant. In this view of construction, facing NW, Redfield House and the opencast plant are visible on the left.
September 1965, A Henshaw

Fig. 50
After leaving Watnall New Colliery the Barber-Walker mineral line continued southwards to the site of the Old Watnall Colliery, crossing the Nottingham-Alfreton road (present B 600) with a branch to a Landsale Wharf beside Common Lane (Frontispiece). At Long Lane, between Watnall and Hucknall, a bridge was constructed over the line, and a platform with a small brick shelter erected beneath the bridge for miners using the Paddy train between Watnall and collieries. This view shows the bridge and platform only, facing north.
The M1 motorway now occupies this site between the Midland Railway's Watnall branch and the adjacent colliery line, a single bridge carrying the lane over the carriageways, replacing the two earlier bridges and short connecting embankment.
January 1955, John R Bonser

KIMBERLEY for Watnall, Nuthall and Giltbrook
134 m 11 1/2 ch

This station and the lines for 1 3/4 miles to the east at Nuthall Sidings must have caused more problems and difficulties for the contractors than any other along their stretch. It involved excavating an ever-deepening cutting, with a tunnel beneath the Nottingham-Alfreton road (present B600), to a summit near the 134 milepost followed by a large area for the goods yard and station itself. This was hewn through hard magnesian limestone with layers of impermeable shale which allowed water to drain freely where exposed. However, the excavated stone was readily trimmed and used extensively in the building of bridges and retaining walls along this distance.

The station buildings were to standard design and built of red brick. In addition there was a brick transit shed on the Down platform, similar to the one at Pinxton, except that the doors were hinged. Another feature was a wooden shed behind the Up side waiting rooms for the use of miners, which lasted into the 1930s. Until the second world war, a cast iron urinal stood on the Up platform beyond the footbridge. No doubt this was removed to assist the war effort, together with railings and the like.

The goods yard was quite spacious, with a large wooden

goods shed and office, also a wagon weighbridge at the eastern end. The usual dock behind the Down platform was extended somewhat for a cattle pen. Beneath the rock cutting at the western end of the coal road stood a replacement timber storage shed for Wm Donnelly which remained in use until about 1950. There was a standard type of hand crane to lift up to 10 tons. Gates beneath the footbridge controlled entrance to the goods yard and transit shed, and between these gates and the main one on Station Road was the usual cart weighbridge and office, together with the lamp room.

The station opened for goods late in 1875. It opened for passengers on 1st August 1876, using a single line only, worked by staff and pilotman between temporary signal boxes at each end. Coal traffic from the Erewash Valley pits was hauled up a 1 in 30 gradient on the north side of the cutting over the top, crossing the Alfreton road on the level, as did Messrs Barber-Walker's line from Watnall Old Colliery. After crossing the road, this temporary line became the Watnall branch from Nuthall Sidings, connecting with the colliery line at Watnall Top, behind the present large bakery. Double line working through the tunnel began in 1877, and on 6th March that year the East signal box was opened to control entrance and exit from the goods yard, from beneath the Kimberley-Watnall road (Newdigate Road) which crossed the deep cutting over bridge 46 (Figs. 56 & 57 p28).

Fig. 51
This view from the Down platform shows an LNER Class J6 64202 ready to leave the station with a passenger train from Derby to Grantham. The neatly kept flower beds on this side, augmented on the Up side by hollyhocks, wallflowers and other flowers which seeded naturally on the sides of the rock cutting gained awards for the Best Kept Station in the area for many years. The building in the right foreground is the Transit shed, Kimberley being the junction station for Pinxton or Derby line trains.
March 1957, H H Mather

The land now sloped down westwards as far as Kettle Bank (now Church Hill) and bridge 48 (Fig.72 p34) but at the station site there were three crossings. First was a footpath from The Flats to Chapel St, needing a footbridge to maintain right of way and used also to connect with each platform by a flight of stairs which was closed and locked with a sliding door on the bridge at night when the station was closed. Second came the old main road from Eastwood which climbed a steep hill (Maws Lane) towards Watnall and descended again past the brewery of the Hardy brothers to join Chapel St. This became Station Road, and crossed the railway on the level at the western end of the platforms. Here the West signal box was built to control the crossing gates. Third was the newer turnpike road, a straighter and shorter route with easier gradients, until the GNR dug it out and crossed it by bridge 47. This needed retaining walls on both sides, and flights of steps connected the lower level to an underpass and Station road above. Station Road was continued on the level eastwards to join the turnpike at an acute angle, which necessitated demolition of the British School on Chapel Street and more retaining walls and boundary walls, all of which were constructed from limestone out of the cutting and goods yard.

Very few properties had to be demolished around the station, but one was a timber storage shed beside the old road at the site of the level crossing, belonging to William Donnelly whose workshops were adjacent. A new access road was made beside the railway's boundary between the footpath at the top and the old road at the crossing.

To the left of the turnpike road reaching as far as Kettle Bank was a large orchard with a few cottages owned by William Hardy, founder of the aforementioned brewery. He lived in one of the cottages himself. The row of four so occupied lay in the path of the railway, and needed purchasing, together with the land, for work to proceed. William Hardy proved very stubborn over terms to part with his strip of land and the cottages. Finally the GNR offered to build him a large house for the portion they needed. "The Firs", as the house was named, was erected in 1874 in the undeveloped orchard which lay between High Street and Main Street. The house and outbuildings included a coachhouse, stabling for three horses and hay lofts (Fig.78 p36) with boiler house beneath. These were connected with a drive from Sydney Street, off High Street, which swept round a right angle to emerge in Orchard Street. A large (steam-heated) conservatory stood opposite the stable block, and steps led down to a pedestrian entrance on Main Street which was developed after the coming of the railway. The steam heating was also continued beneath the drive to warm the main rooms downstairs in the house, the pipes being inside cavity walls.

Fig. 52
A typical mixed goods train with Class B headlamps struggling up the steep incline caused by subsidence at bridge 48, behind an Ivatt class J6 0-6-0. The rather grandiose station nameboard reads: 'Kimberley for Watnall, Nuthall and Giltbrook' 'Change for Pinxton and Derby Trains'.   *c. 1950, H H Mather*

The GNR having acquired the cottages and land, demolished two of the cottages to build the line and kept the other two to house their own employees (Fig.61 p30). Fig shows the south side of the house with its fine stained-glass window illuminating the staircase and the entrance on the right. The two cottages which became GNR property are seen extreme left. Entrance to the house is beyond the coachhouse. The Firs was later used partly as a private residence, but with the ground floor as a private nursery until 1988. The Town Council applied to have the building listed. However, before this was passed, the roof was removed and the building demolished within a week. The orchard is now occupied by elderly warden-assisted homes. The Firs is replaced with a large building of similar flats named Maple Court.

In 1917 Bridge 46 was replaced due to damage caused by water allowing the weight of stone and rock to slide inwards on the impervious shale. The replacement abutments were of blue brick, and the cross girders of steel. The parapet was steel plates, and beneath the east footpath was a 12-inch water main and a gas main. Shortly after this, the East signal box, opened as required by a porter-signalman for the use of the goods yard only, was demolished and replaced by a three-lever Ground Frame on the same site. This was released by a lever from the West box which was renamed simply 'Kimberley'. Single needle telegraph was installed along the line, worked from the signal boxes, in March 1883. Up goods trains upon passing, would whistle a code indicating their destination to be telegraphed forward: 2 long for the Old Bank (Goods Reception); 3 long for Main Line at Colwick to Carlton Fields. 1 crow (long/short/long/short/long) meant the train was for Bulwell Common GC.

Sidings covered for commercial purposes by Kimberley were Lodge Colliery, Erewash Valley Brick Pipe and Pottery Co's Digby siding, New London and Digby Collieries, Nottingham Corporation Giltbrook Chemical Works, Watnall Colliery, Watnall Public Siding (for goods traffic), and Nuthall Sand Sidings of Stanton Ironworks Company. Goods traffic/ Farm traffic by the wagon load was taken to and from Watnall Wharf by B.W. colliery engine from the goods road (Frontispiece Map).

The yard was shunted during the afternoon by the 'Sand Train'. This left Leen Valley Junction at 1.02 pm with traffic for stations to Ilkeston together with empty low-sided (3 plank) wagons. The train was shunted inside the sand siding at the Ground Frame by the Watnall shunter. Loaded wagons of sand for Stanton Works were exchanged for the empties before the train left for Kimberley. Here, in addition to shunting the yard the wagons of sand were weighed.

Fig. 53
The Down side platform, buildings and connecting footbridge as seen from the signal box. Sliding barriers at the top of the steps were drawn across when the station was not open for traffic. Reboilered LNER Class O4 hauls a train of mineral empties from Stanton to Colwick.

August 1962, A Henshaw

The train called at Awsworth Junction if needed, and Ilkeston, where more shunting was done before a load of traffic for Stanton was booked to depart for the Works at 6.00 pm. Before leaving for Stanton Works, the crew would be relieved by men travelling from Netherfield on the 4.46 pm passenger train to Derby. The second crew were booked to work a train from Stanton Works at 8.55 pm to Bulwell Common GC.

The two major industries in the town were brewing and hosiery. The two breweries of Messrs Hardy and Hanson were both served by private sidings from the Midland Railway which ran between them, and they amalgamated in October 1930. Ale traffic for Lincolnshire and the East Coast resorts was despatched from the GN station, the wagons being attached to Burton-Colwick trains by arrangement with Control. Parcels and small goods consignments were carted to the outlying villages by farmers who had milk rounds in Kimberley. Passenger traffic was mostly commuters to the hosiery factories at New Basford and Nottingham together with office workers. Less traffic was booked westwards, except on Saturday, when there was a rush of passengers to Ilkeston for Market Day. As along the Pinxton branch, seaside excursions were well patronised, especially between the wars.

After nationalisation British Rail renamed the goods depot Kimberley East on 1st July 1950, and the passenger station Kimberley, replacing the large nameboard with a smaller enamelled one on 13th June 1955. This was hardly necessary, for passenger services from the Midland station had ceased from 1917 and the track between Kimberley and Bennerley Sidings lifted after 1920.

Sunday passenger services on the GN route ceased after 11th January 1962, and all passenger services followed suit on 7th September 1964. On 2nd November of that year the station was closed to all traffic. The signal box remained open to work the crossing gates, and act as an intermediate block post between Basford North and Ilkeston East for through trains to Stanton and Derby westwards via Egginton Junction until May 1968. The track was recovered and taken to Stanton for disposal in January 1970.

Before through running ceased, the goods yard site and station buildings were bought by Charles Manson & Sons, timber merchants, who erected several large storage sheds between bridge 46 and the footbridge which has been replaced by another steel structure supported on a central concrete pillar in March 1991.

The cutting, Watnall tunnel and railway land to Hempshill was bought by Broxtowe Borough Council, and used for disposal of non-industrial waste, largely from the upgrading and renovation of housing estates in the area. After settlement during 1981, a caravan site was provided on the land west of the Alfreton Road (B600) over Watnall tunnel for the use of residents from Nuthall Larkfields, whose aluminium prefabricated homes were being replaced with permanent homes on the same site. In 1991 a housing development was being built on the empty caravan site, but between there and bridge 46 the contractors have excavated the infill, sifted and riddled it as a precaution against a build-up of methane gas. This has led to drainage water collecting at the bottom; the GNR drains beneath the trackbed being smashed by removal of the rails! This housing venture has failed.

The trackbed west of the infill beside the old goods yard has been made into a 'GNR footpath' with metal plaques indicating its former use. The drainage stream has been dammed to form a pond near the footbridge and the platform area has been cleared, drained and metalled to form a small car park with new wooden gates at the entrance and a small industrial unit on the north side.

Bridge 47 was demolished in 1987 and the site over the underpass is now occupied with a large house and garage accommodation, and the stairway entrances from the main road blocked off.

Fig. 54
A similar view to Fig. 52 p25 from east of the footbridge (46A) shows the Up side waiting rooms, and a much diminished nameboard in vitreous enamel stating 'Kimberley'. Immediately beyond the Level crossing is bridge 47 with the Main Street beneath. The Up Home signal is reduced to driver's eye-level height, and the branch distants on the Up side seen in Fig.71 p34 are missing, having been removed during the period of the 1914-18 war.

c.1963, H H Mather

Fig. 55
A Stanier Class 8F and brake heading towards Kimberley from the west end of 268 yard tunnel. Kimberley's Up advance starter is on the left. The diamond plate on the post indicates that the track is circuited, and the telephone to the signal box is in the box beyond.
July 1966, A Henshaw

Fig. 56
Due to the weight of rock above slipping inwards on layers of shale above narrow coal seams, the original bridge became unsafe and was replaced in 1917 with this plate girder structure seen from the east side. This was always called locally 'New Bridge' and still exists despite the cutting and tunnel to the east having been filled in with waste, which also envelops the bridge. The distant arm is no longer beneath the outer home signal, which is track circuited to indicate when a train (invisible from the signal box at the platform end) is standing there. The box at the foot of the post houses a 'phone connected to the signal box Notice the loading gauge at the eastern end of the Goods Yard. The East signal box was replaced with a Ground Frame to allow entrance to and exit from the Goods Yard.
c.1914, Courtesy British Rail

Fig. 57
Kimberley East signal box which controlled entrance to the Goods Yard, nestles into the cutting beneath the original bridge 46, constructed of stone quarried from the cutting, as were several more in this vicinity. Note the very long stove pipe chimney to counter downdraught. Beside the Down home signal post is the fogman's hut for the West Box's distant.

May c.1904, H H Mather

Fig. 58
A view of the timber goods shed and adjoining Goods office seen from the Down platform. The wagon weighbridge was at the east end of the shed, and it was here that sand quarried at Nuthall for Stanton Ironworks was brought for weighing and charging.
The two sidings on the extreme right served coal merchants and a timber/joinery works whose storage shed stood in the corner near the footbridge.

c. 1965, H H Mather

Fig. 59
The typical Derbyshire Extension 5-10 ton goods yard crane seen from the dock. A BR Class 2MT 2-6-0 is approaching the station with a short train for Derby.

August 1962, A Henshaw

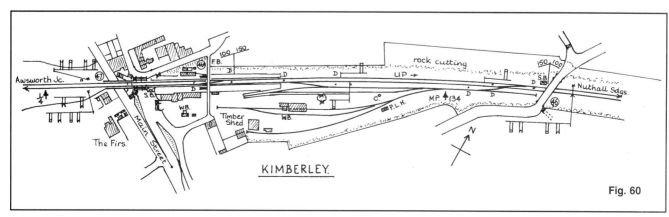

KIMBERLEY.

Fig. 60

Fig. 61
A sorry sight with platform edges missing and the Up side in ruins, but so late in the life of the line was the level crossing renewed. This Sunday morning shot shows the engineers in possession of both running lines. Beyond the crossing, left of the signal post can be seen a pair of railway cottages whose access to Main St beneath the bridge was *via* a tortuous flight of stone steps.

May 1966, A Henshaw

Fig. 62
Looking towards the station from bridge 47, this view reveals the stepped approaches from Main Street to the Down side and underpass. There was a gas lamp on the gritstone capping beneath the noticeboard. Top right are seen the Railway Cottages near the end of the footbridge, now without its corrugated sheeting, and below them the weighbridge office and gate at the station entrance. Similar steps from the other side of the bridge connected to the Up side of the crossing.

May 1966, A Henshaw

Fig. 63
The station approach from Chapel Street, formerly Chapel Bar before the turnpike road was lowered, which shows the different levels necessitating the stone retaining walls for connecting Station Road at the Level Crossing to the turnpike (Main Street). The track at the crossing was being relaid at this time, hence the stationary brake-van on bridge 47.

May 1966, A Henshaw

Fig. 64
Considerable construction was necessary on the approaches to Kimberley Station, involving three distinct levels. Fortunately a ready supply of magnesian limestone was available from the cutting and goods yard excavations for dressing and building. This view shows Main Street left dipping beneath bridge 47, and Station Road diverging to cross on the level and lead to the station entrance. The natural level of the ground slopes down from Barnes' Hill to the right.

May 1966, A Henshaw

Fig. 65
This old postcard shows a group of Wm Donnelly's workmen in aprons standing in Main Street near its junction with Station Road which leads to the crossing gates beyond. An up passenger train is passing, the last vehicle being a 6-wheeled brake. The building beyond the bridge 47 is the Great Northern Hotel, the left hand side of which was built from the lower road level. The stone retaining walls between the road levels show clearly, and the patch of ground beyond the building on the right is clearly cultivated.
before 1906, Courtesy A Plumb

Fig. 66
A closer view of bridge 47 and the underpass beside which could be used by pedestrians when the wicket gates at the crossing were locked. The building immediately beyond the bridge is the lower remains of the former Great Northern Hotel (burnt down in July 1940), and beyond the car is the former MR Goods Shed, once used by the local brewery. On 31st May 1944 it was burnt down and demolished shortly afterwards.
May 1966, A Henshaw

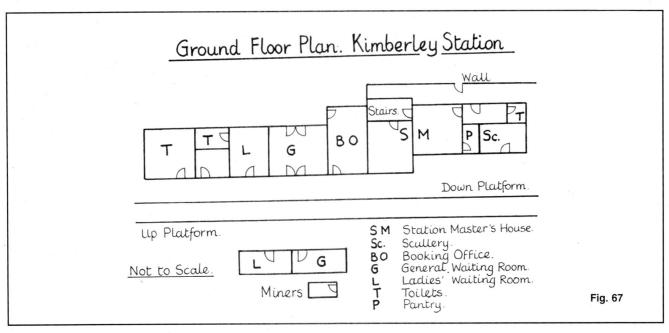

Ground Floor Plan. Kimberley Station

S M   Station Master's House.
Sc.   Scullery.
BO   Booking Office.
G   General Waiting Room.
L   Ladies' Waiting Room.
T   Toilets.
P   Pantry.

Fig. 67

Fig. 68
This view of Kimberley Station shows Ivatt Class D3 4-4-0 1316 with a light train of 6-wheeled coaches passing through at speed. The engine carries passenger express headlamps, and a 'Newark' destination board on the smokebox indicating that it is most probably the 11.55 am ex Derby Friargate, which called at Ilkeston, Nottingham Victoria, London Road High Level, Netherfield & Carlton and Radcliffe-on-Trent, before arriving in Newark at 1.13 pm.
The signalman has been quick to open the crossing gates to road traffic. The branch distant for the Pinxton line is seen to the right of the Signal box. The tall post of the Up Home signal on the opposite side held a 'sky arm' so that good visibility in daylight was ensured before passing bridge 48 at Kettlebank. The end of the Transit shed is on the left.
c. 1907, late F H Gillford

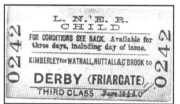

Fig. 69
An early photograph of Stationmaster George Charles Pike, on the left, who was appointed from Leicester in 1912 and remained at Kimberley until his retirement in 1932, when he was succeeded by Mr J M Reddish. Later still, his son G Frank Pike became Stationmaster at Kimberley until its closure, and resided at the Station House (no longer owned by Charles Manson and Co), after his retirement from the railway.
Courtesy F Pike

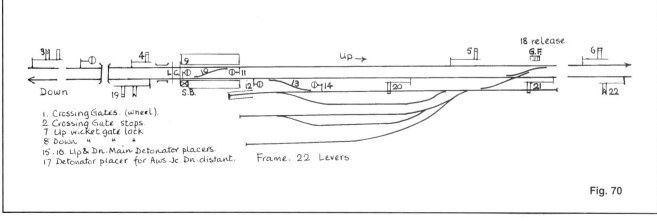

1. Crossing Gates. (wheel).
2. Crossing Gate stops.
7. Up wicket gate lock
8. Down "   "
15.16. Up & Dn. Main Detonator placers.
17. Detonator placer for Aws. Jc. Dn. distant.

Frame. 22 Levers.

Fig. 70

Fig. 71
This enlargement of the view through bridge 48 reveals features of the station not remembered by the author. Reading from the left, the home signal protecting the crossing has a 'sky arm' repeater above, and beneath it is the East signal box distant, painted red, and without chevron. After the grouping of companies in 1923, distant arms were painted yellow, with a black chevron. The white boards on the footbridge are notices for passengers to cross the lines by the bridge. Beyond the much foreshortened platforms can be seen East signal box and its home signal. Right of the signal box is the tall post and bracket holding the down starting signals (repeated) and extra distant for the Pinxton line. The road is signalled for the Main line to Ilkeston at Awsworth Jcn. The pair of railway cottages above Main Street are seen further right, together with the 134 1/4 mile post which is behind the signal wires.
c. 1904, Courtesy British Rail

Fig. 72
Bridge 48 west of the station, carrying the old High Street of Kimberley up the steep Church Hill known locally as Kettle Bank, a name taken from the nearby Kettle Brook. Note the use of stone from the cutting, and compare with Fig.73
c. 1904, Courtesy British Rail

Fig. 73
Two additional brick piers now support girders carrying the Derwent Valley water main from Langley Mill to Swingate and an additional bracket is seen beneath the bridge. On the left is the Banner type repeating signal installed in LNER days to replace the earlier sky arm which protected the level crossing.
July 1966, A Henshaw

Fig. 74
The block instruments, track circuit indicators and diagram above the levers. The mirror at the left hand end reflected the road scene at the gates. Hanging on the window frame to the left of the circulars are point clamps and lever collars.

May 1968, A Henshaw

Fig. 75
The back interior of the signal box with the wheel for opening and closing the crossing gates in the foreground, and the signalman, Jack Taylor, recording entries in the Train Register Book. Although later wired for mains electricity for lighting and power, an older oil lamp remains as a stand by. The duster on the mantelpiece above the stove (right) was invariably used when pulling levers, and for cleaning up at the end of a shift.

May 1968, A Henshaw

Fig. 76
This detail of the interior of the signal box shows the Saxby & Farmer rocker lever frame with locking mechanism behind. The large number of spare (white) levers indicates that there are no longer any points or sidings worked. The levers with chevrons work emergency detonator placers (known as fogging machines, since a detonator was also called a fog signal).
Note the lever collars on numbers 17 and 20. The wheels on the right adjusted tension on the signal wire for No.21, Down outer home, and 22, the Down distant. A corner of the signalman's lockers is visible on the extreme right.

May 1968, A Henshaw

Fig. 77
The Firs. The house built in 1874 by the GNR for Mr William Hardy who lived in one of the row of cottages to the left in what was then an orchard. A very noticeable feature of this southwest side is the stained glass window which illuminates the broad staircase. It was removed from the British School on Chapel Street when it was demolished for the extension of Station Road to join the Main Street, and depicts the four ages of man; childhood, youth, maturity and old age. Since demolition of this fine house, the Local Historical Society, with assistance from the Council and others has purchased the window and mounted it in the Parish Hall. The ground floor was used as a private nursery school as shown by the decorations on the window, right, until it was sold for development of old people's homes, demolished and replaced by a new building named Maple Court. The railway cottages are extreme left.
March 1985, A Henshaw

Fig. 78
Shows the Stable block and coach house seen from Orchard St. The weathervane had the monogram 'H' for Hardy worked into the design. Entrance to the house is beyond the coach house. 'The Firs' was then used as a private nursery school
March 1985, A Henshaw

Fig. 79
The gates beneath the footbridge at the entrance to the Goods Yard, formerly occupied by a large timber merchants, who evacuated the site at the end of 1996, since when it has been sold to Broxtowe Borough Council. The roadway between the gateposts was lowered for access of high loads. Note the oil tank beside the transit shed, left. This site is now cleared for the building of further homes for the elderly, and includes conversion of the single storey buildings on the Down platform (Feb 2000).
August 1973, A Henshaw

Fig. 80
Facing west towards Kimberley, the impressive depth of the cutting is clear. The Down outer home signal protecting the crossover is near the site of the original East signal box (Fig.57 p28).

May 1966, A Henshaw

Fig. 81
The now disused Goods Yard and dock seen from the footbridge across the station. Stanier Class 8F 48388 is passing with a train of coal for Stanton.

May 1966, A Henshaw

AWSWORTH JUNCTION   134 m 62 1/4 ch

When opened on 23rd August 1875, this signal box did not operate as a junction, because the Main line through Ilkeston to Derby and Egginton was still being built. This showed in the allocation of levers until about 1930; numbers 1, 2 and 3 pulling the Down distant, branch Home signal (5 on the plan) and branch starter (6 on the plan) respectively. The small yard, for dealing with exchange traffic between Pinxton line stations and the Derby line consisted of 3 sidings on the Up side of the Main lines, with an arrival road and run round loop from the Pinxton branch.

The yard was shunted by the 7.10 am Colwick-Pinxton Pick-up, and an afternoon trip was made from Digby sidings as necessary. Later traffic to be picked up for GC routes

via Bulwell Common would be left on the line behind the signal box when no shunter was on duty.

The yard closed along with stations on the branch on 7th January 1963, but the signal box remained open for the last coal traffic from Eastwood until 16th May 1966, after which the windows were boarded up as a protection against vandalism. It was finally demolished after the tracks were lifted in 1970.

The footpath beyond the station was broken with the removal of bridge 47. Bridge 48 has been filled in and a few houses built on its east side in the original cutting. West of here the GNR footpath continues, provided with seats, a signal post and upper quadrant arm, together with numerous informative metal plaques as far as bridge 51 at Awsworth Lane where steps lead down to the road.

Fig. 82
A good view of the signal box and shunter's cabin with a very long stove pipe. Rain water was collected in the butt for washing purposes. Drinking water was brought from Kimberley station on the Down pick-up and filtered before use. An ex-LMS class 4F 0-6-0 is working up the gradient with the Summer season Saturday only King's Norton to Skegness express.

c.1960, S Holmes

Fig. 83
The view approaching Awsworth Junction from Kimberley. The three yard sidings are on the right with the miniature signals for controlling shunting movements. No.16, the top one invariably pulled off to allow internal shunting past the signal box. On the left are the Main lines, with the Down home signals and Platelayer's hut. When Awsworth Station signal box was open, there was an Outer distant arm beneath the one on the Main post.

July 1966, A Henshaw

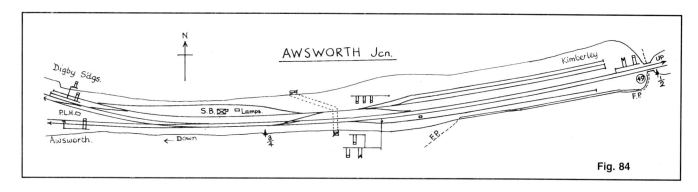

AWSWORTH Jcn.

Fig. 84

Fig. 85
The junction and signal box, boarded up against vandals since closure of the Pinxton branch, facing east from the branch. A Stanier 'Black 5' 4-6-0 No. 45004 heads a train of empty oil tanks from Colwick to Ellesmere Port. Note the British Rail plywood-faced platelayer's hut. The miniature signal 25 on the left beside the arrival road controlled exit from the yard to the branch.
July 1966, A Henshaw

Fig. 86
The view from between the lines of the Up branch from Pinxton, with a train of empty petrol tanks from Colwick to Ellesmere Port running down the Main line. The entrance to the arrival road is on the right, with disc signal 26 for crossing over to the Down branch close by. The author remembers the Up Main home signal in the centre as a very tall post with a 'sky' somersault arm at the top to give better daylight visibility to men working up the 1 in 89 gradient (originally 1 in 100) from Awsworth.

July 1966, A Henshaw

Fig. 87
A detailed shot of a GNR-type disc or ground signal controlling the exit from the Down shunt siding.
June 1955, A Henshaw

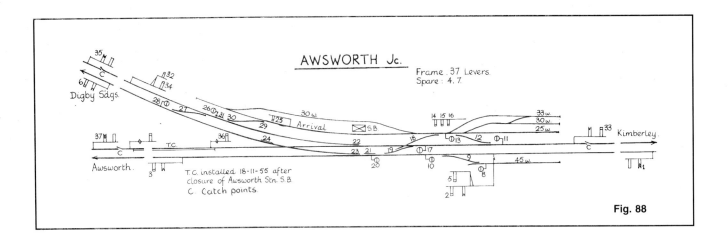

AWSWORTH Jc.

Frame. 37 Levers.
Spare : 4, 7.

35

C

6

Digby Sdgs.

32
34

28 27   26 31 30   30 w.
                29   25   Arrival   S.B.   14 15 16   33 w.
                                                                     30 w.
37   36   24   25 w.
          T.C.   22   18   13   12   11   C   33   Kimberley
          C   23 21   19   17
Awsworth.   20   10   9   45 w.
3   5   8
                                                     2

T.C. installed 18-11-55 after
closure of Awsworth Stn. S.B.
C. Catch points.

Fig. 88

Fig. 89
The Giltbrook viaduct seen from the first coach of a Nottingham-Pinxton passenger train which has passed over the junction points. The Up branch home signal 34 is 'off' for a train from the branch to pass, and above the buffer stops is the hawthorn-covered embankment of the Midland Railway's route from Bennerley Junction to Basford.
c.1960, C A Hill

Fig. 90
Looking west from the signal box, the sharp curve from the Main lines before the continuing gentle swing of the viaduct can be seen. In the foreground is the run round road behind the signal box, where GC traffic for Bulwell Common would be left for an easy pick-up. Awsworth Lane runs between the two hedgerows, centre, above which is the overgrown embankment of the Midland Railway's Bennerley Junction to Basford branch. Above this arch, bolted to the parapet, can be seen the Down branch starting signal post and its stay post opposite.
August 1965, A Henshaw

3. GILTBROOK VIADUCT - PINXTON

THE GILTBROOK VIADUCT 134 m 78 ch to 135 m 24 ch

Officially bridge 1 on the branch after Awsworth Junction, this magnificent structure, the largest of its kind on the Derbyshire Extension, was built in under two years between 1873 and 1875 of, it is believed, locally hand-made red bricks.

It followed an S-curve in plan, first to the right, and more gently to the left at its northern end. There was a string course of bullnose shaped blue bricks, and the parapet was recessed above each pillar, capped with a gritstone coping.

The foundations were of rubble masonry, concrete-mortar and rubble masonry in mortar: there was a total of 28,050 cubic yards of brickwork and masonry of which 13,760 were built by 1st November 1874, and the remaining 14,290 completed by the summer of 1875. The pillars had a batter of 1:32, and the width between parapets was 25 ft 8 ins. Drainage was provided by an 18-inch square catchpit of 9-inch brickwork above, discharging through a 6-inch cast iron pipe under each arch. In severe winter weather huge icicles would form on the end of these pipes. Filling above the arches was of burnt colliery shale at the north end, and of quarry waste (magnesian limestone) from the cutting

and goods yard at Kimberley at the other, waterproofed with a thick layer of bitumen.

The first arch spanning the Awsworth Lane from Kimberley to Ilkeston was a large skew structure to which a substantial embankment abuts. Arches numbers 8 and 23 were strengthened by building four storeys of dwellings, which had windows, plastered walls, and fireplaces whose flues had cast iron chimney pots at the top. Arch number 15 was skew, to the south side of which was incorporated arch number 44, beneath which was an access road to the Chemical Works, and above it an embankment carrying the Midland railway's branch from Bennerley Junction to Basford. Beneath arch number 31 was the Midland Railway's earlier mineral branch to Speedwell Colliery, and leaving this to the left was a line into Digby Colliery yard which ran beneath another skew arch, number 32. Number 35 arch spanned the Greasley arm of the Nottingham Canal (which was fed from the Giltbrook) and was segmental, being of 45 ft span, with an 8 ft 6 in span on either side, that on the western side for the towpath.

The dwellings inside arches 8 and 23 were used by the bricklayers and workmen during the construction, and temporarily by schoolchildren from Awsworth during World War I when German Zeppelins came over to drop bombs in the area of Bennerley and Stanton Ironworks.

Fig. 91
A view of the viaduct from the site of the chemical works showing ex-LNER class L1 tank engine 67748 with the 4.15pm Nottingham-Pinxton passenger about to cross the Canal arch. The skew arch beneath the third coach spanned the Midland Railway branch to Digby Colliery, and the adjacent one spanned the Speedwell Colliery branch.
March 1961, R W Sheppard

Fig. 92
This view of the north-east face as seen from Awsworth Lane shows the dwellings in the eighth arch in some detail, and the embankment of the Midland Railway's Bennerley to Basford branch removed from beneath the fifteenth arch. A good sense of scale is gained from the Austerity 2-8-0-hauled coal train to Colwick, most probably from Eastwood.
September 1959, John R Bonser

This grand, graceful but massive viaduct was a landmark for miles around, and when closed with the last of the Pinxton branch on 2nd November 1964 was scheduled for preservation as a building of historic interest. However, to make way for the new A 610 by-pass from Nuthall to Langley Mill, with a junction for the Kimberley-Ilkeston road it was demolished in the spring and summer of 1973, but not without hitches. The 'square' arches along most of its length were broken through by a crane on each side of the pillars swinging a heavy ball. On the very first occasion, a misty Sunday afternoon, March 11th, the cranes swung into action north of arch 23 with the dwellings built in. Once the arch was broken through the pillar to the south, lacking pressure on the arch, slowly cracked and fell over, breaking the next arch, and so on back to arch 23 which stood firm. The crane driver on the north side, not anticipating such hasty results, had not swung his crane jib out of the way, and it finished a crumpled mess beneath the heaps of masonry! Trouble was also experienced with skew arch number 1 over Awsworth Lane. Here dynamite and shot powder were used, and as a precaution, the road beneath the arch covered with 5 feet of soil as a protection for water pipes beneath the road. The first explosion blew a small hole in the abutment to the embankment revealing vaulting of neatly laid brickwotk inside. Three hours later a larger detonation made a bigger hole, and damaged some of the pillar on the other side of the road. Later still the cranes were brought into action to smash through the arch, still intact! A few hours later in the afternoon it was broken, and the cranes attacked the remaining brickwork until the arch was removed. The rubble from the viaduct was used as hardcore filling for the road construction nearby.

Fig. 93
A shot from the brake van of the Austerity-hauled coal train from Eastwood to Colwick as it climbs the 1 in 100 gradient over the viaduct towards Awsworth Junction. This view shows the northeast side and the Up branch home signal 34 in the 'off' position beside the miniature arm 32 on the bracket beside it. The hawthorn bushes in the foreground cover the disused Midland embankment of the Bennerley Junction to Basford branch.
August 1965, A Henshaw

Fig. 94
A detailed shot of the two arches which spanned the Midland branches to Digby and Speedwell collieries. Through the skew arch is a stack of opencast coal, and the colliery office building. Like Watnall, this was another site for loading opencast coal for rail transport.
August 1958, A Henshaw

Fig. 95
The more gentle curve at the northern end is seen here from the embankment, erosion of which round the fencing post reveals the large bull nosed bricks of the string course. Beyond the first field is the line of the Greasley arm from the Nottingham Canal, now reduced to a drainage ditch, beyond which, occupying the land where the chemical works stood is the yard of Whitehead's concrete works where slabs and fence posts were made after 1948. The access road along this side of the viaduct shows up clearly.

March 1973, A Henshaw

Fig. 96
This shows the graceful canal arch looking north with the two smaller arches beside. The one on the left had the towpath. The channel was made into a drainage ditch with flood banks now hardly discernible through growth of reeds and tall plants.

*November 1972,
A Henshaw*

Fig. 97
Awsworth Lane beneath the first arch, showing the girder bridge 51 carrying the Main lines to Awsworth with the Gate Inn on the right.

July 1958, A Henshaw

Fig. 98
A detail of the brick drainage chamber in the centre from the bottom of which led a 6in diameter iron pipe beneath the arch, projecting some 3ft away from the pillar. The recess in the parapet wall and coping stones are also included.

March 1973, A Henshaw

Fig. 99
Viewed from the other side the skew arch shows clearly against the normal square ones, through which can be seen the embankment of the Midland Railway.
August 1958, A Henshaw

Fig. 100
Demolition of the first arch over Awsworth Lane, showing the effect of the first explosions and the small amount of brickwork removed because of the vaulting inside the abutment and the first pillar. Note the heaps of earth protection.

April 1973, A Henshaw

Fig. 101
The second explosion at around 12 noon certainly removed more of the first pillar, but the arch stood firm, and despite the covering of earth beneath, the water main was broken by a block of brickwork dropping above a valve, which cut off the supply to Awsworth village for a few days.

April 1973, A Henshaw

DIGBY SIDINGS   135 m 47 1/4 ch

Four collieries were served by the GNR from Newthorpe station, Digby, New London, Speedwell and Lodge. Traffic from all of these was dealt with at Digby Sidings, a wooden signal box perched on the embankment at the northern end of the Giltbrook Viaduct, beside the Down line.

Digby Colliery Company owned the first three; Speedwell Colliery was last worked in 1887 being merged with Digby, and used to raise water from the workings there until the 1920s. New London, near the village of Newthorpe was served by a colliery line from Digby which crossed the Nottingham- Eastwood road on the level, and ran beside the Giltbrook for approximately half a mile. Earlier still, a tramway from a pit in Watnall Wood had used this route to reach the Nottingham Canal's Greasley arm. Lodge Colliery

was sunk on the east side of the GNR lines, and opened in 1878. It was called locally 'Billy Hall's', and the Midland Railway had no access to this traffic.

The Digby clay pit of the Erewash Valley Brick Pipe and Pottery Company was originally served by a siding north of the signal box, possibly removed when the brickworks was reached by sidings from Newthorpe.

On the southwest side of the Giltbrook Viaduct, beside the Greasley arm of the Nottingham Canal was a chemical works of the Nottingham Gas Light and Coke Company. This was already served by the Midland Railway's mineral branch from Bennerley Sidings to Digby, but traffic via the GNR could be worked over the colliery line to the GNR sidings.

Digby and New London collieries had closed by 1937,

Fig. 102
A view from the branch to the colliery, showing the NE face of the viaduct, and loaded and empty wagons standing on the branch lines. Immediately above the empty wagons is the Greasley Arm of the canal with loaded wagons beside it. Further on are more wagons on the sidings to the Midland Railway lines, with the embankment of the Bennerley-Basford branch beyond them.
*c.1905,
Author's Collection*

Fig. 103
A box camera view of the signal box facing Awsworth Junction from beside the Down Main line. The loaded end-door wagons are on the branch to Digby Colliery which fell away steeply to the left behind them.
c. 1938, E Painter

but the Ministry of Fuel and Power took over the site at Digby in 1940, erecting a screening plant to deal with opencast coal from the area. This traffic was brought out of Digby Sidings in large quantities.

Lodge Colliery, under the National Coal Board after 1947, was merged with Moorgreen in 1960 and demolished by 1966.

On 23rd April 1957, hot ashes from the engine of the 5.10 pm Pinxton to Nottingham Victoria passenger train working up the 1 in 100 gradient to Awsworth Junction set fire to the dry grass around the base of the signal box, and it was burnt to the ground, there being no ready access for emergency services As a temporary measure, block instruments were placed in a Platelayer's hut on the Up side, and traffic controlled by handsignals. A ground frame soon replaced this arrangement for access to Lodge Colliery from the Up Main line. Empties for the pit were then worked to Eastwood, where the engine would run round its train and return to Digby to dispose of them.

No visible traces now remain of these collieries. The Digby site is occupied with a connecting road from Giltbrook to Awsworth, and slip roads to the A 610 by-pass. Further north is a modern industrial estate of single-storey units. Hall's Lane, which led to Lodge Colliery from Newthorpe Common skirts a modern housing estate which reaches the industrial estate. The A 610 by-pass construction swallowed up Newthorpe station, although the factory which stood behind it is still there and in production.

Fig. 104
A view of the wooden signal box and its young signalman, unfortunately unidentified. The small wooden coal bunker seems to need replenishing.
c.1937, Courtesy A Plumb Collection

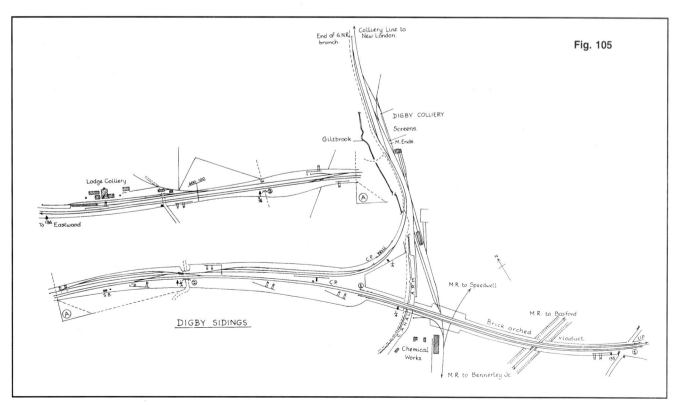

Fig. 106
Although Digby Colliery was dismantled in 1937, coal was still being worked from Lodge Colliery, the points being worked from a ground frame. This view taken from an Eastwood-Colwick coal train passing the site of the signal box shows the curve of the Giltbrook viaduct and the embankment carrying the Main lines to Awsworth and Ilkeston to the right.
August 1965, A Henshaw

Fig. 107
This view from beside the Up Main line shows the siding to Lodge Colliery. The short siding on the right is where the brake van was left before empties were pushed up to the colliery sidings. The signal post opposite the colliery buildings once held Digby Sidings Down starter, but now only Newthorpe's Distant signal is visible on it.
June 1963, J A Evans

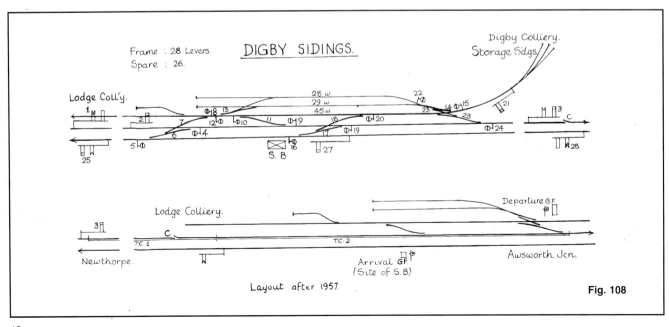

Fig. 108

Fig. 109
The guard's view passing Lodge Colliery, half dismantled, with a coal train from Eastwood to Colwick, hauled by a WD Austerity 2-8-0 loco.
August 1965, A Henshaw

Fig. 110
A view of Digby colliery yard facing north towards New London Colliery, also worked by the Digby Colliery Co. The screens are to the left. Between the two miners in the foreground is the roof of the colliery offices at the foot of Gilthill where the branch to New London crossed the Nottingham-Eastwood road (old A610). The buildings behind the wagons on the right are workshops, etc. The last building, between the wagons, was the First Aid room.
*c. 1930,
L Bradley Collection*

Fig. 111
A Digby Colliery shunting loco 'The Verney'. Judging by the waste tips in the background, this photograph is at New London Colliery. Note the cleanliness and good condition of the engine. Built by Avonside Engine Co in 1891, number 1345, this engine began work at Pleasley Colliery. After a rebuild it went to Holwell Ironworks in 1924 and NCB No 2 Area in January 1947, working at Whitwell until being scrapped in 1948. A similar engine was loaned to the Bennerley Ironworks during the 1930s because of the regular failure of their one and only shunter. Its driver, used to propelling three or four loaded wagons of slag up the ramp to the crusher, and often failing to reach the top, was amazed at the efficiency and capability of the Digby engine!
c.1937, E Painter

NEWTHORPE AND GREASLEY for SHIPLEY GATE
136 m 40 1/2 ch

This station was built where the road from Eastwood to Shipley Gate crossed the line over bridge 6. The main buildings were of standard design built of red brick on the Up platform, the approach being from the north side through a gate which also led to the Goods Yard. The platforms were half staggered, and connected by a latticed footbridge near the end of the Down platform, the signal box being situated at the opposite end this platform upon which was the small wooden waiting rooms building on a brick base.

Just to the northwest of the station, in a field between the Erewash and Nottingham Canal was the small Eastwood Colliery, originally owned by a Doctor Manson but soon taken over by Messrs Barber & Walker. The pit was served by a single line branch from Shipley Gate on the Midland Railway which crossed the Erewash canal by a timber bridge. Coal being the main object for building their line,

the GNR built a short branch to this pit through the two arches of bridge 6. The lines came together to cross the Nottingham Canal by a swing bridge alongside a similar bridge for road traffic. However, the colliery closed around 1884 due to underground water. The small wagons of up to 8 tons capacity would have been brought over the canal by horse. No trace of the pit remains, but the site, still known locally as Manson's field, is overgrown with hawthorn and bramble and the embankment leading to the Nottingham Canal is still there. A note on the GNR plans of 1903 states: " Thos Barber and Elizabeth Campbell compensation damage to land £300" – presumably this small embankment!

After closure of this colliery the branch was singled ending in a buffer stop, and the swing bridge removed. Close beside was built a stout brick shed with a thick concrete roof known as the 'Powder Shed'! Mr J H Skelton, a chemist whose shop was opposite the 'Sun Inn' of Midland Counties Railway notoriety dealt with explosives for the local miners.

Fig. 112
A view of the station facing south east from overbridge 6 (Mill Lane) which shows the main station buildings behind. Just leaving the Down platform is the 4.15 pm from Nottingham Victoria, behind LNER class L1, 2-6-4 Tank 67758.
May 1960, R W Sheppard

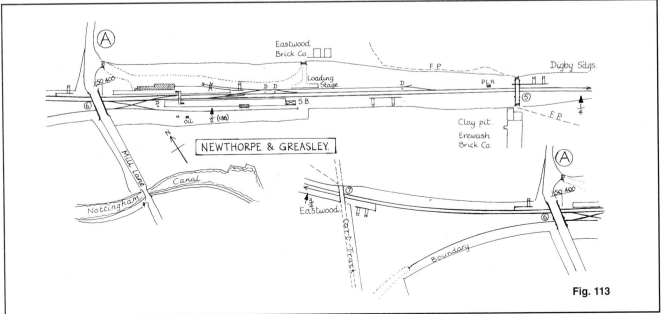

Fig. 113

The vans of dynamite in sticks and gunpowder were not dealt with at Eastwood, but at Newthorpe. Explosives stored in this shed, well away from the station and other buildings, were distributed by horse and cart to surrounding pits. Although the powder shed was removed earlier, the siding remained until the period of the second world war.

Clay is plentiful close to the coal seams, and many collieries had their own brickworks. There were brickworks on both sides of the line at Newthorpe. That on the north side was owned by the Eastwood Brick and Pottery Company, and on the south side was the Erewash Valley Brick, Pipe and Pottery Company. The two companies later amalgamated to form the Manners Brick Company,

and private sidings served the works on both sides. On the north side, sidings also served the works of the Wilkins Wire Rope Company, opened 1939, later Birnam Products, a subsidiary of Tinsley Wire Ropes Ltd. Wire springs for beds and chairs were made here, and were sent in containers to the Ford Motor Company at Dagenham. Shunting within the works was by wire haulage rope wound by electric capstan.

The station was closed to passenger traffic on 7th January 1963, and to goods traffic on 16th May 1966. The buildings and bridges were demolished for construction of the A 610 by-pass to Langley Mill in 1973.

Fig. 114
A young Mr E (Teddy) Painter poses in the doorway of his signal box. Mr Painter was Porter Signalman at Newthorpe at this time. Note to the right of the picture the row of houses on the road into the Brickworks, visible because the Wire Rope factory was not then built.
c.1937, E Painter

Fig. 115
Standing at the edge of the Down platform is an unknown young porter with a bandaged right wrist. Of more historic interest are the wooden privately-owned colliery wagons behind which stands one of the brick kiln chimneys.
c.1935, E Painter

Fig. 116
An enlargement of the view through bridge 5 looking north, and showing several somersault arms, so distinguishing a feature of the GNR before amalgamation in 1923. Behind the oak fence on the left embankment was the siding to the Brickworks. The signalman is evidently interested in the photographer, who has his tripod between the rails of the Up Main line, whilst all signals are off for a train on the Down! Behind the wagons is the loading gauge gantry at the exit to the dock. Immediately behind the bridge abutment can be seen the balance weights and pulley wheels for the Up starter and Digby sidings distant arm, beside which is a typical sleeper-built platelayer's hut with a brick flue for use by the fog signalman when stationed at the signal.
c.1904, Courtesy: British Rail

Fig. 117
The footbridge, No.5B connecting the staggered platforms, showing the track layout as in Fig.122, with bridge 6 beyond. The short branch to Eastwood Colliery (Fig.3 p3) passed beneath the two arches to the left.

c.1904,
G Dow collection

Fig. 118
The approach to the station from Mill Lane showing the rear of the buildings and station house with the upper storey rendered; the only one of its type to have this treatment against damp.

June 1963, J A Evans

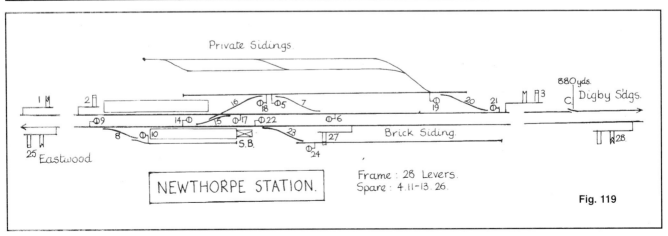

NEWTHORPE STATION.

Frame : 28 Levers.
Spare : 4.11-13. 26.

Fig. 119

Fig. 120
The typical, but not standard, wooden waiting rooms erected along most of the stations along the Derbyshire Extension. The smaller room with fireplace and one window has been changed from 'Ladies' to General Waiting Room.

June 1963 August 1966, J A Evans

121
An evening view of the 6.56pm passenger train from Pinxton to Nottingham entering the station with but one member of staff to deal with it. Note the footbridge number plate 5B, 5A being a culvert beneath the station and rails.

1951, F Quenby

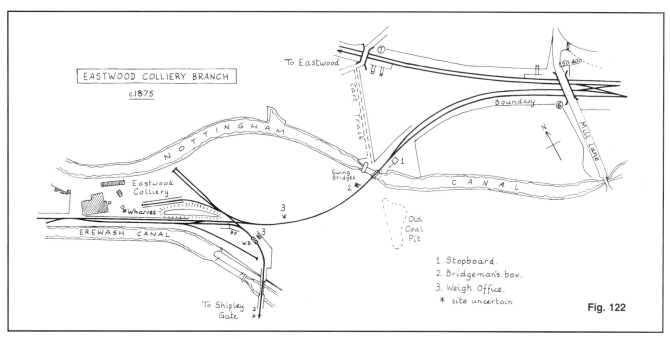

EASTWOOD COLLIERY BRANCH

c.1875

To Eastwood

NOTTINGHAM

Cart Track

Boundary

Mill Lane

CANAL

Swing Bridges

Eastwood Colliery

Wharves

ERE WASH CANAL

Old Coal Pit

W.B.

To Shipley Gate

1. Stopboard.
2. Bridgeman's box.
3. Weigh Office.
* site uncertain

Fig. 122

EASTWOOD and LANGLEY MILL 137 m 42 1/2 ch

Opened with the lines to Pinxton on 23rd August 1875 for goods and mineral traffic, and 1st August 1876 for passenger traffic, this station varied from the standard design. Hugging the hillside on which Eastwood stands, the line is in a shallow cutting between bridges 8 and 9. Bridge 8 carried Bailey Grove road over the railway; and beside the road were two GNR cottages and the Stationmaster's house, a detached dwelling close to the east of the bridge. Two more pairs of employees' cottages were built on the west side towards the Nottingham Canal. Bridge 9, a substantial red brick structure carried the Nottingham-Heanor-Ripley road (A 610) over the railway as well as the Booking/Parcels Office and Hall. In 1913, the Notts and Derbyshire electric trams were inaugurated between Ripley and Nottingham and the girders beneath the roadway were replaced with steel and brick jack arches, and beneath the south footpath was laid a 2-ft diameter water pipe from the Derwent Valley. The width between the parapet and the Booking Office was 38ft.

The platforms were opposite, reached by covered staircase from the Booking Hall above the bridge. Brick-built waiting rooms and toilets stood on each platform near the stairway entrance. The rather squat North signal box was situated at the north end of the Up platform, controlling the workings to and from Messrs Barber & Walker's extensive colliery lines.

The large goods yard occupied the land between bridges 8 and 9, and was served from the Main lines by the South signal box on the Up side near bridge 8.

This box was normally closed, and opened as required by a porter/signalman when the pick-up called. The commodious brick warehouse and goods shed had a wagon weighbridge with office at the south end, and the main office at the north end. A hand-worked crane of standard design for the Derbyshire Extension stations had a capacity of 10 tons. The usual road weighbridge and office were situated near the entrance gate off Derby Road, and a stable with manure pit was also built beneath the embankment to the road, for in addition to the general goods traffic from

Fig. 123
Looking south from the Down platform this view shows a group of passengers awaiting an east coast excursion, and bridge 9 with stairways to each platform from the booking hall. The waiting rooms are brick built. Note the GNR-type somersault signals 27 and 18 Fig.128 p56.
c.1920, R Hull collection

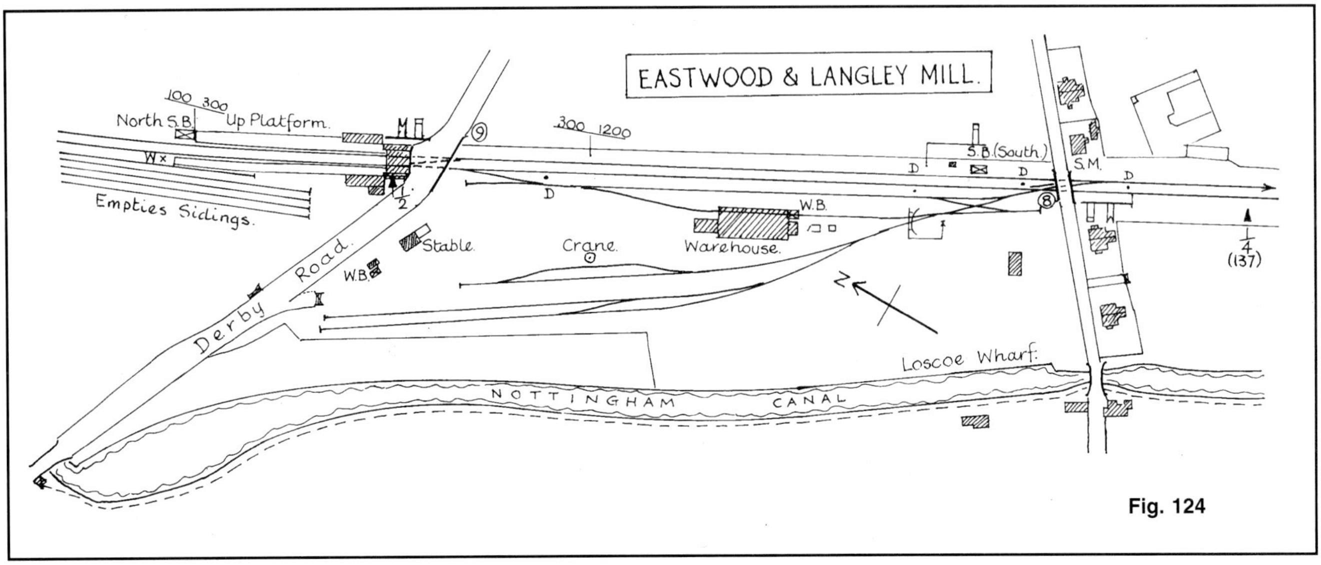

Fig. 124

surrounding hosiery factories, agricultural and grain traffic was dealt with by the wagon load and the cartage service covered a wide area. Messrs Barber Walker controlled most of the collieries in this area, and had a considerable network of railway lines connecting them, reaching from Underwood (later renamed Pye Hill No 2 by the NCB) and Moorgreen to Watnall, with Landsale wharves at Brinsley, Newthorpe (Dovecote Road) and Watnall. A garage and filling station on the B600 road occupies the site of the last-mentioned wharf. To transport miners between the various pits along these private lines Barber Walkers ran their own paddy train which consisted of a few four- and some six-wheeled coaches with wooden seats, hauled by one of their six-coupled tank engines, usually immaculately clean and well maintained. A short spur from near Watnall Wharf crossed the Midland Railway (originally serving Watnall Old Colliery) to join the GNR Watnall branch from Nuthall Sidings.

Eastwood North signalman had block bell communication with the colliery company's Beggarlee signal box, which controlled traffic to and from the Midland Railway at Langley Mill as well as the GNR. There was a code of engine whistles for leaving the Downside empties sidings for Beggarlee, the number of whistles being repeated on the block bells between the two signal boxes (Fig.127 p56). Entrance to the colliery lines was protected by a signal 7 beside the Main line bridge above (Fig.129 p57).

In 1905-6 H A Ivatt's 0-8-2 tank engines (GNR Class L1, LNER R1) designed with small driving wheels for rapid acceleration with heavy suburban passenger trains from King's Cross were not a great success in London, and were sent to Colwick and the West Riding for working goods and mineral trains. To keep these engines supplied with

sufficient water when working along the Pinxton branch, a pumping house and water tank was built beside the Nether Green brook which was culverted beneath the tracks. Water was drawn from this brook, and water columns situated at the departure end of each platform. These class R1, or 'Baltic' tanks as they were locally known, also worked the afternoon miners' train along the branch.

An annual event which incurred heavy livestock and agricultural traffic was the Moorgreen Show, which is still held on August Bank Holiday, now at a permanent ground in Watnall. Excursions to the east coast resorts of Skegness and Mablethorpe always proved very popular between the wars, with most of the passengers arriving but a few minutes before the train, which would be standing in the platform whilst a frantic booking clerk was still issuing tickets to a line of people on the pavement outside!

The station was closed for passenger traffic on 7th January 1963 along with the branch stations beyond to Pinxton, but was kept open for coal traffic from Moorgreen until May 1966.

Nothing now remains, for the A610 by-pass from Junction 26 of the M1 at Nuthall to Langley Mill occupies the site between Lodge Colliery at Newthorpe and the station. Opened as a dual carriageway in Spring 1976 it has been extended to join the older dual carriageway between Langley Mill and Codnor to accommodate heavy coal traffic from a large opencast site at Godkin. The extension took place in 1982-3, and reaching its eastern edge is a huge spoil heap from Moorgreen Colliery which closed in July 1985. At least the large hill is covered in grass!

Fig. 125
LNER class L1 2-6-4 Tank 67769 enters the station with the 6.56pm passenger train from Pinxton to Nottingham Victoria. The pump house chimney, water crane and North signal box are seen more clearly here.
June 1959, W R Sheppard

Fig. 126
A scene at Moorgreen Colliery with a former Barber Walker 0-6-0 tank engine at the Engine Lane level crossing, looking east towards High Park. 21 was built by Kitson's (works no 3501) in 1891 and went new to Barber Walkers at Moorgreen (Eastwood) as No 4. Under the NCB it was transferred to Denby Hall in 1953, returning to Moorgreen in 1958 until being scrapped in 1961. The chimney and dome have a distinct H A Ivatt look. The washing plant hopper and screens are on the right.
September 1959, John R Bonser

Fig. 127
An NCB saddle tank 0-6-0 21 shunting in the colliery sidings at Eastwood with the Barber Walker Beggarlee signal box in the centre of the picture behind the water crane. Considerable coal traffic was dealt with here from the several pits linked with the Barber Walker mineral lines, and during the second world war, trains of empty Private Owner wagons from Woodford to Annesley were diverted to Eastwood when necessary to overcome a shortage of supply from Colwick.
November 1955, John R Bonser

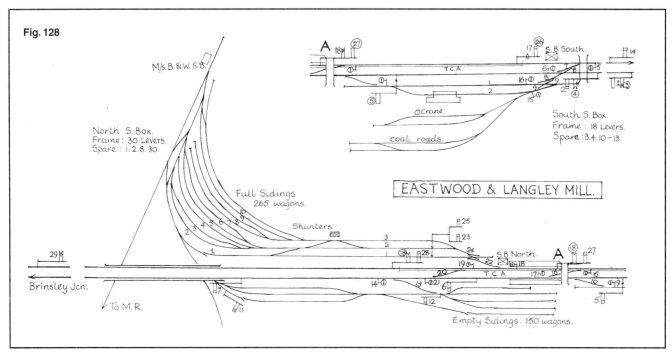

Fig. 128

EASTWOOD & LANGLEY MILL.

Fig. 129
This close view of the wrought iron girder spans at the south end of viaduct 11 shows a colliery 0-6-0 saddle tank passing signal 7 to continue beneath the span, through which can be seen the line from the full sidings to the Midland's Beggarlee branch from Langley Mill. The Colliery Workshops appear through the second span.
Designed by Riddles for the Ministry of Supply in 1943, these locomotives saw much service in France until the end of the war, afterwards being purchased by railways (LNER class J94) and the NCB for use at collieries. Built by Hunslet in 1944, works no 3190, it came to NCB Area 6 at Moorgreen Colliery in October 1947 as NCB 9.
November 1955, John R Bonser

Fig. 130
The main civil engineering work along the mineral lines of Barber Walker collieries occurred between High Park and Watnall pits where the railway climbed the escarpment which overlooks the ruins of the once Carthusian Beauvale Priory, beside which the line had passed. Here a standard NCB 0-6-0 saddle tank is hauling a train of internal user wagons up the gradient beneath a stone arched bridge which gave access to forestry land to the east.
March 1955, John R Bonser

Fig. 131
A forlorn view of the station minus track and the North signal box. Notice the mineral wagons in the Down empties sidings which were still used by the NCB for Moorgreen Colliery. Although the bridge remained until the by-pass was extended in 1982 the buildings were demolished shortly after this photograph was taken.
September 1969, A Henshaw

Fig. 132
Derby Road, Eastwood, facing Langley Mill, showing the Booking Hall and Parcels Office above Bridge 9. The roof of the stairway to the Up platform can be seen above the hawthorn shrubs and further right still is the roof of the waiting rooms. The A610 by-pass to Codnor now occupies the site, with an elevated roundabout immediately to the left.
September 1969, A Henshaw

Fig. 133
The signalman's view as a train of coal is marshalled in the full sidings. One wagon, centre, stands on the Up main line.
c.1953, J Fretwell

Fig. 134
The North signal box and station seen from between the Main lines in the late evening. On the left is the outlet from the full sidings controlled by the miniature signals (23 and 25, Fig.128 p56), behind which is the shunter's cabin and sleeper-built platelayer's hut. A train of empty wagons is on the right.

c.1960, J W D Miller

Fig. 135
The offices and west side of the warehouse showing the awning over the loading area. The South signal box is to the right, beyond which is the Co-op bakery.
August 1965, A Henshaw

Fig. 136
Between bridges 8 and 9, south of the station was the goods yard, the entrance to which was controlled by the South signal box. This view shows the south end of the warehouse with the weighbridge office. In the background right, can be seen the cart weighbridge office and stable building.
August 1965, A Henshaw

Fig. 137
The view from the station bridge 9, facing south which shows the cottages on the left, and the Station master's house on Bailey Grove. The South signal box is no longer there. This has become the line of the A610 by-pass.
September 1969, A Henshaw

Fig. 138
A detail of the hand crane base. At the bottom of the jib casting a flangeless wheel rested on the bevelled edge of the base plate. When turned by the toothed wheel above it, the crane rotated. The brake handle on the right tightened a metal strap round the wheel beneath the chain and hook, used to hold the handle up to release the brake, and a pawl with ratchet at the other side secured any load. A steel chain was wound round the drum for lifting, and was used singly for light loads, or double, through a pulley block for heavy loads. The plate on the base of the jib reads 'To lift not more than 6 tons single chain and 10 tons double chain'. It was made by Kirkstall Forge Co., Leeds, in 1874.

March 1967, A Henshaw

Fig. 139
The standard type of goods yard hand-worked crane seen along the Derbyshire Extension line, now minus chain with pulley block and hook.
August 1965, A Henshaw

Fig. 140
This early picture is a pre-grouping view of the station and buildings facing south just including the name board on the Down platform (extreme right). Right of the Up side stairway the water column is faintly visible with the signal posts and arms. How clean and tidy are the platforms and buildings – even the trackbed and rails.

A Knighton collection

Fig. 141
Signalman Barry Roberts with his means of transport to and from work outside Eastwood North signal box between workings. Most signalmen and shunters in this area used cycles or motorcycles to travel to work because of shift workings. Barry was later transferred to Nottingham London Road station to work the Goods Yard signalbox.

February 1953, B Roberts

Fig. 142
Eastwood shunter Charlie Barksby, left, with the Porter signalman, who in addition to his platform and other duties, opened and operated Eastwood South signalbox as and when required by the pick-up goods to shunt the goods yard. Note the re-railing ramp on the left against the fence.

February 1953, B Roberts

STONEY LANE 138 m 29 3/4 ch

Before the coming of the GNR a tramway carried traffic from Clinton Colliery and brickworks to the nearby Cromford Canal for distribution further afield. On opening on 23rd August 1875, a signal box was built to control the level crossing, and a siding provided on the Up side for traffic from this pit which was opened by James Oakes & Co prior to 1853, and closed by 1887. The brickworks remained in production until the early 1900s. After the colliery closure, the signal box was replaced with a ground frame with a wooden cabin for the crossing keepers. The site was closed with the rest of the branch north of Eastwood on 7th January 1963.

Fig. 143
The signal box and a part of the crossing gate open for the road. This shows the south end and steps, along with the signalman. The handles on the wheel to operate the gate movements can be seen through the window opening. The large bracket on the top rail of the gate was for a lamp with a red glass, probably removed temporarily for cleaning and refilling. The track in the foreground with early type of ballasting which covered the sleepers, was the Down Main line. Stoney Lane connected Brinsley with the Cromford Road at Aldercar (old A610) and crossed over the nearby Cromford Canal. The Working Timetable dated 1912 shows the signalbox closed nightly between 6pm and 8am (1800 hrs to 0800 hrs) and all day on Sunday

c. 1904, P Stevenson collection

Fig. 144
Before 1900 Clinton Colliery and brickworks stood beside Stoney Lane to the east of the GNR, and had been served by a narrow tramway to the Cromford Canal at Clinton Wharf. Bridge 12 spanned this tramway when the line was built and was rebuilt in 1906 This view is facing east towards the brickworks, and shows the hut at Stoney lane.

c.1904, Courtesy British Rail

Fig. 145
An early photograph of the signal box and level crossing it controlled seen from the Up siding. Note the new type concrete signal post, still with the somersault arm.
c.1910,
Author's Collection

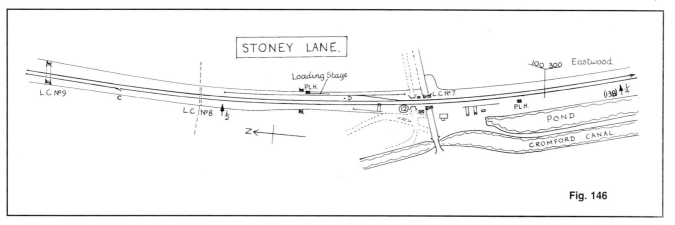

STONEY LANE.

Loading Stage

P.L.H.

L.C. Nº9

C

L.C. Nº8

Z

P.L.H.

L.C. Nº7.

100 300 Eastwood.

(138)

POND

CROMFORD CANAL.

Fig. 146

POLLINGTON SIDINGS 138 m 72 1/4 ch

Pollington Colliery, opened in 1876 by James Oakes & Co, was famous for sending one huge lump of coal weighing 4 tons 12 cwt to a Colliery Exhibition in London in the year 1903.

It was reached from the Midland Railway by a branch over which the GNR passed. Connection to the GNR was to the Up Main line through four double-ended sidings from the colliery branch. The colliery was closed in 1926, after which the signal box was closed.

After commencement of the Second World War in 1939 the Ministry of Fuel and Power re-opened the colliery site and installed screens for loading opencast coal to wagons. A new signal box was built, and equipped with modern signalling apparatus to deal with the traffic. Empties to, and loaded out of here were dealt with by the Eastwood men making trips as necessary during the afternoon shift, loaded wagons being taken 'rough' to Eastwood and marshalled with the Eastwood traffic for Colwick, or Bulwell if routed *via* the Great Central. The signal box was manned by a signalwoman, but little came of the venture, and after several months the signal box was closed again.

Fig. 147
Bridge 13 carrying the road to Brinsley Hall over the railway, facing north.
c.1904, Courtesy British Rail

Fig. 148
This enlargement of the view through the arch of Bridge 13 shows clearly the hump in the track beneath which the Midland Railway branch to Pollington passed. Note the somersault signals, and the bracket near the engine with a distant signal for the branch at Brinsley Junction. This directing distant signal was removed around the end of World War I.

c.1904, Courtesy British Rail

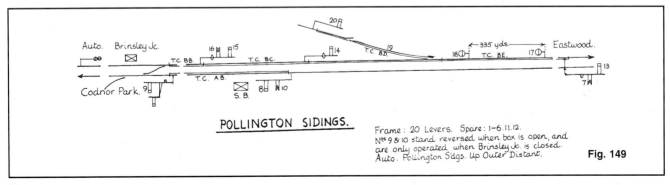

POLLINGTON SIDINGS.

Frame: 20 Levers. Spare: 1-6.11.12.
Nos 9 & 10 stand reversed when box is open, and are only operated when Brinsley Jc. is closed.
Auto. Pollington S'dgs. Up Outer Distant.   **Fig. 149**

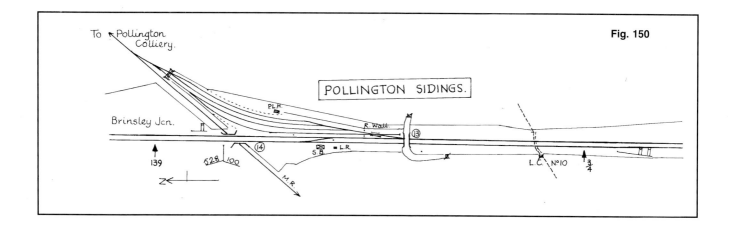

Fig. 150

POLLINGTON SIDINGS.

BRINSLEY JUNCTION 139 m 40 1/2 ch

This signal box, some distance from road access, controlled the short branch of 39 chains to Codnor Park Ironworks of the Butterley Company, a large and prosperous firm already served by the Cromford Canal and the Midland Railway. Although less than half a mile in length there were four bridges along it, the last one crossing the canal before joining the sidings into the works. The first bridge was an occupation arch. Number 2 was a timber viaduct crossing a footpath from Westwood to Codnor and the River Erewash, and carrying a single line track only. To control this change from double to single line, and the sidings, Brinsley Sidings signal box was built at the eastern end of the viaduct on the embankment. Bridge 3 was a brick semi-circular arched construction over a stream, the Bagthorpe Brook, which joined the River Erewash lower downstream.

The branch was opened after the lines to Pinxton in 1876, being inspected on July 29th of that year.

To maintain running powers over the Midland lines to New Mills, the branch was extended beyond the Ironworks sidings to join the slow or goods lines of the Midland Railway at Codnor Park GN Junction, because of the damage to the viaduct previously connecting the lines at Pye Bridge (see Fig.179 p76)

The original signal box was replaced in 1899 for through working to the Midland lines, and inspected on April 11th 1900. At around 1940 the branch was singled throughout, and Brinsley Sidings box closed, being replaced by a Ground Frame, released by Annett's Key from Brinsley Junction, for access to the Ironworks.

Colliery subsidence has always been a problem along the Erewash Valley lines of both the GN and Midland Railways, and the lattice girders of bridge 4 were replaced by wrought and cast iron girders between the two wars. Engines allowed to cross the timber viaduct were restricted to 0-6-0 wheel arrangement, but on one occasion during the last war a train of petrol tanks from Ellesmere Port to the depot at Redmile was routed *via* the Midland lines and Brinsley Junction. Colwick men relieved the Midland crew at Codnor Park GN Junction, to find it was hauled by an LNER O4 class 2-8-0! Having no alternative but to bring the train they worked it safely to Redmile and returned engine and brake to Colwick, to be sharply reminded of their transgression by the shed foreman!

Inwards traffic for Butterley Forge sidings was brought from Colwick on the early train of empties for Pye Hill, the signalman from Codnor Park opening the box for this purpose. Outgoing traffic was dealt with in the evenings, the shunter booking on at 5.30pm. Colwick traffic was shunted and cleared with the engine from the 6.55pm passenger train from Nottingham Victoria to Pinxton after stabling the stock, and the engine and crew from the last Pinxton passenger train cleared the GC traffic into Bulwell. The express goods train, 8.22pm from Manchester Deansgate to Colwick was worked by Trafford Park enginemen with a Deansgate guard, who were relieved at Colwick upon arrival, to return with the 1.03am ex-Colwick to Deansgate. On the approach of the Up train, the engine working at the sidings would be recalled over the single line to the junction until the train had passed. If during the war the Up train was delayed unduly (a frequent occurrence) Colwick men would bring the 1.03am Down to Eastwood where the crews would change over.

The branch was closed in 1954 due to the deterioration of the bridges along its length. Codnor Park GN Junction signal box closed on July 4th, Brinsley Junction a day earlier, but the last working of the Deansgate Goods was on 12th September 1952 by engine s64832.

The trackbed south of Codnor Park is well lined with trees and bushes, and used as a footpath, and by horses and youthful motor-cyclists as far as the bridge at Pollington, which has been removed, together with those along the embankment of the Brinsley branch to Codnor Park GN Junction. The only exception along this stretch is the culvert for the Bagthorpe Brook, No 3, and the abutment and pillar of the canal bridge 4, on the east side of the canal.

Fig. 151
This is the only photograph of the location the author has been able to trace. Like Digby Sidings, the construction was of wood, and had the usual small coal bunker. The view is taken from the Down Main line facing southeast.
April 1957, P Stevenson

Fig. 152
Bridge 16 (Fig.153) just north of Brinsley Junction facing north with the Down starter signal 3 on the left. Note the spectacle plate at driver's eye-level, below the signal arm.
c.1904, Courtesy British Rail

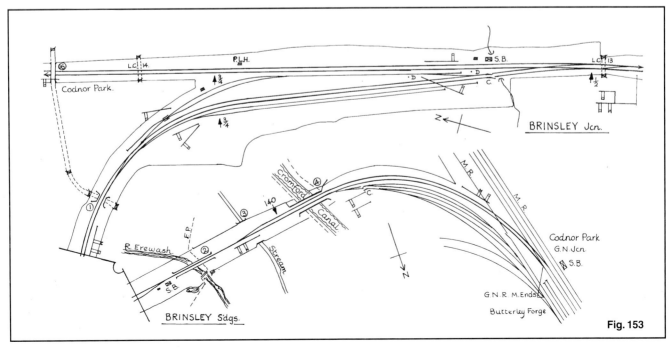

Fig. 153

Fig. 154
The Midland Railway signal box on the Erewash Valley line which controlled the branch to Brinsley Junction. This curved away to the left beyond the telegraph pole, from the Goods lines which are furthest from the signal box.
September 1955, J P Wilson

Fig. 155
The same signal box as Fig.154 above, looking NE showing an ex-LMS class 4F with an up freight train. The signal arm controlling the branch has been removed from the right-hand post.
September 1955,
J P Wilson

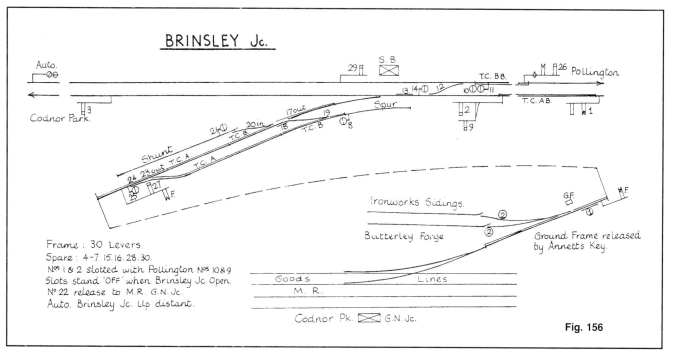

BRINSLEY Jc.

Frame : 30 Levers.
Spare : 4-7.15.16.28.30.
Nos 1 & 2 slotted with Pollington Nos 10&9
Slots stand 'OFF' when Brinsley Jc. Open.
No 22 release to M.R. G.N. Jc.
Auto. Brinsley Jc. Up distant.

Fig. 156

Fig. 157
Before reaching the Midland Company's lines, the branch crossed the Cromford Canal by bridge 4. The South side is seen here, facing Brinsley Junction. Note the signals (shown in Fig.153 p66). The lower, distant arm is painted red, without the later white chevron.

c.1904, Courtesy British Rail

Fig. 158
Brinsley viaduct, bridge 2 on the branch to the Midland Railway at Codnor Park. This timber structure spanned the River Erewash and a footpath. Note the stone retaining wall. The signal box on the right is Brinsley Sidings which dealt with traffic from Codnor Park Ironworks.

c.1904, Courtesy British Rail

Fig. 159
A view facing West towards the Midland Railway's lines along bridge 4 over the Cromford Canal, with the single line *in situ*.

April 1957, P Stevenson

Fig. 160
The two spans over the canal and footpath of bridge 4 have been replaced by wrought iron girders seen from the footpath side, facing the Midland Railway. The central timber support would appear to be original.

May 1967, A Henshaw

CODNOR PARK 140 m 35 ch

This exceptional station opened for goods/mineral traffic on August 23rd 1875, and for passengers on August 1st one year later. Originally called Codnor Park and Selston, it was renamed simply Codnor Park on May 22nd 1901. Later still it became Codnor Park for Ironville and Jacksdale, and finally Jacksdale in BR days, to distinguish it from the Midland Railway's Codnor Park station.

The station was built on a brick arched viaduct and the platform buildings were of wood on both sides, reached by a covered staircase from a subway with a lift from street level to the Up platform. The booking and parcels office were at street level under two of the arches. The original platforms with stone surfaces, were extended southwards as far as the bridge over the canal basin to accommodate longer trains of commuters to hosiery factories at New Basford and Nottingham, and the holiday excursion trains to the east coast. These extensions had timber surfaces. The Station master's house was a detached building beside the road which passed under the railway, north of the platforms. The goods yard approach was almost opposite it. There was a brick-built goods shed with adjoining office,

a road weighbridge and office, and a crane with a 5-ton lifting capacity.

Signal boxes under the supervision of this station were Codnor Park, Brinsley Junction, Brinsley Sidings and Pollington. Works sidings dealt with were Codnor Park Brinsley Ironworks; Butterley Company's Ironworks; Brands and Brittain Collieries; James Oakes & Company's Alfreton Ironworks; Riddings Colliery and Brickworks; Riddings Sanitary Pipe works; and Pollington Colliery. Although considerable traffic was generated by these industries, it must be said that the Midland Railway, having established itself in 1847-8, took the larger share.

The station was closed to all traffic on 7th January 1963, after which demolition of the bridges and buildings took place in 1974.

The trackbed south of the canal basin is used as a footpath and by horse riders and youthful motor cyclists as far as Pollington and Stoneyford, but the bridges have been removed, as have those along the branch from Brinsley Junction to Codnor Park, except for the culvert, bridge 3. The pathway is flanked on either side by a good crop of 20-year old trees.

Fig. 161
GNR class E1 2-4-0 705 heads a Pinxton-Newark train as it pauses at Codnor Park. The destination boards on the smokebox were normal practice on the GNR prior to the 1914-18 war. Note the wooden platform on the viaduct, the two milk churns and hand trolley on the Down platform and the gas lamps. A clean and tidy station! Above the Down side parapet, faintly discernible in the distance, can be seen a goods train passing Codnor Park Junction on the parallel Midland Railway.
c.1910,
Author's Collection

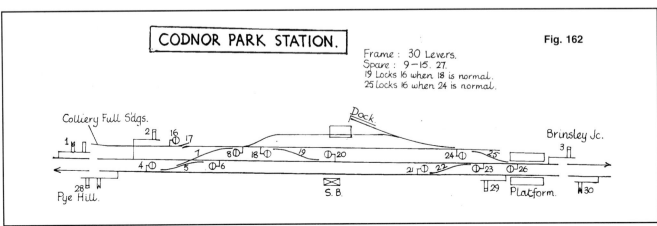

CODNOR PARK STATION.

Fig. 162

Frame : 30 Levers.
Spare : 9 — 15. 27.
19 Locks 16 when 18 is normal.
25 locks 16 when 24 is normal.

Fig. 163
LNER class L1 2-6-4 Tank 67758 with the 6.56 pm Pinxton to Nottingham Victoria train. Note the gradient post beyond the platform ramp, the wooden extension of the Down platform and the change from gas-lit lamps in Fig.164
June 1960, R W Sheppard

Fig. 164
A fine view of the viaduct 21, (Fig.165) on which the passenger station was built, seen from the southern end. The first arch (right) had a skew span of 35ft 4in. The next two were skew with spans of 17ft 7in, followed by two square spans of 20ft. The wider section consisted of 13 spans of 20 ft each, followed by a brick segmental arch of 20ft, and lastly a brick segmental skew arch of 28ft 8in over the Selston to Ironville road. The rear of the Down side shelter and station nameboards can be seen together with the oil-lit lamps.
c.1904, Courtesy British Rail

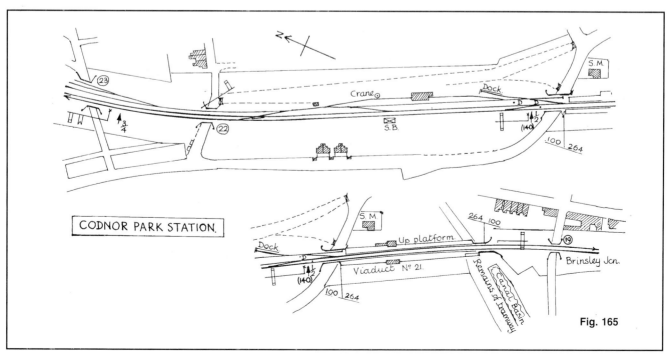

CODNOR PARK STATION.

Fig. 165

Fig. 166
The small goods yard with its loading dock, cattle pen and warehouse was situated north of the station (Fig.165 p71). This picture shows the loading gauge above the dock and the warehouse to he left.

June 1963, J A Evans

Fig. 167
An aerial view of the Butterley Company's works at Codnor Park in the lower half of the picture separated from the village of Jacksdale by the meanderings of the River Erewash. Westwood village is in the top left corner.

The GNR station on viaduct 21 is on the left above the broad river bed. To the right is the canal arm to Portland Wharf from the Cromford Canal which forms the boundary of the works. Nearly adjacent is Stone Row built by the Butterley Company along Jacksdale Street from the canal locks to the wharf.

The forge works which produced high quality wrought iron and later with rolling mills narrow gauge tubs for collieries and standard gauge railway wagons, were closed in 1965. Stone Row and the rest of the works were demolished in the 1960s, the wharf having been filled in ten years earlier.

The Midland Railway which forms the lower boundary reached here in 1847 and extended to Mansfield a year later. Note the Butterley Company's mineral line crossing into the works where the locomotive of the empties train has just passed. The wagons are still passing Codnor Park (MR) station. Left of the station approach road is Forge Row, also built by Butterley. *(no date), Author's Collection*

Fig. 168
The north-facing view of the elevated platforms and waiting rooms in pre-grouping days. In the haze beyond the platforms is the signal box and home signals on one post with separate spectacle plates lower down. On the Up side a locomotive is standing at the signal box close to the loading gauge and dock.
A Knighton collection

Fig. 169
This shows the station approach from the street. Two brick arches with windows house the booking and parcels office. The staircase leads to the Up platform, and a lift shaft was provided for heavy parcels traffic.
June 1963, L Little

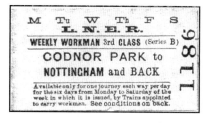

Fig. 170
A wintery scene facing south showing the plain enamelled BR nameboard, and chimneys removed.
Winter 1963, D Mather

PYE HILL 141 m 19 1/2 ch (2nd Station)

The original station which opened for all traffic on 3rd April 1877 was a small one with opposite platforms, built to the south of a junction which connected to the Midland Railway's Erewash Valley lines at Canal Junction. The land to the west of the valley drops steeply here, the GNR hugging the hillside in a cutting, the spoil from which provided the bed for four sidings on each side of the branch, which then crossed the Nottingham-Alfreton road (present B 600) and the River Erewash by a brick viaduct of six arches 1 (Fig.179 p76) The approach to this station was from beside the viaduct, skirting Pye Bridge MR station, and the GN Station House was built beside the road on the east side of the viaduct. Severe subsidence so damaged this structure that despite timber strengthening the branch was closed in 1899, and the arches demolished.

A new station was built 280 yards north of the original one, and the sidings beside the branch removed to make room for the goods yard. A new approach led from the road near bridge 26 to the Up platform, passengers for Pinxton crossing the main lines on the level. The platform buildings were of timber with slate roofs, but the goods shed was brick with awnings either side. In 1906, this

station was renamed Pye Hill and Somercotes.

A connection from the Up side led to the Pye Hill and Selston collieries, but empties only for these pits were handled here. The loaded coal was brought out at Codnor Park.

Between Pye Hill and Codnor Park the lines from Pye Hill and Selston Collieries curved sharply to the north and south to connect with the adjacent Midland Railway Erewash Valley lines. These curves were bridged by Oakes' viaduct 24. The connections from James Oakes' colliery and pipeworks at Riddings passed beneath the Midland Railway with much less clearance than normal; beneath the GNR with more clearance, and joined the colliery branch from Pye Hill beyond bridge 25 (Figs.173 & 174).

After closure and demolition of Pye Hill station, except for the goods shed, the site was used by a firm of earth-moving vehicles and heavy plant, but they have now gone, together with the goods shed and bridge 27. To the north, the trackbed remains beneath bridge 26, beyond which the area east of the Midland lines and the River Erewash is being opencast mined for coal, obliterating all traces of the railway towards Pinxton (August 1999).

Fig. 171
Because of the lower level of the Midland lines in the foreground, the colliery branch to Riddings had unusually low clearance in passing beneath. Two of the colliery locos, No.11 a Hunslet no 1493 of 1925 and a Barclay 705 of 1891 are seen here cut down for clearance to about the size of the 13-ton wagons behind them. The GN main lines crossing bridge 25 are behind (Fig.183 p78).

May 1964, R C Riley

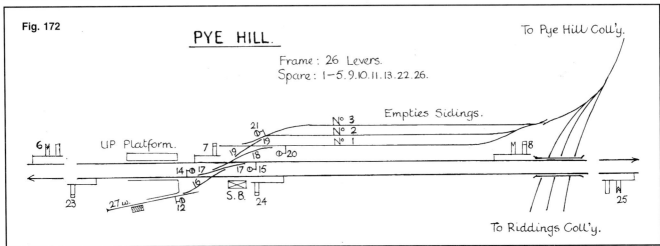

Fig. 172

PYE HILL.

Frame: 26 Levers.
Spare: 1-5.9.10.11.13.22.26.

To Pye Hill Coll'y.

To Riddings Coll'y.

Fig. 173
Between Codnor Park and Pye Hill stations the GNR and MR ran almost parallel and quite close together, with the GNR hugging the east side of the valley at a higher level than the MR. Both railways had connections to the numerous collieries, pipe and ironworks of James Oakes in the vicinity. This photograph of Oakes' viaduct 24 shows the line from the GN empty sidings to Pye Hill Colliery in the foreground. The wagons stand on the north curve. In the hazy distance between the right hand telegraph pole and the lamp standard is the tower of the monument to William Jessop Junior of the Butterley Company who died in 1852. *c.1904, Courtesy British Rail*

Fig. 174
The view of bridges 25 and 25A between Pye Hill and Codnor Park stations, looking west. In the foreground is the sleeper-fenced footpath beneath the colliery branch from Pye Hill, the lines of which appear right and left of the brick pillars. Just behind is bridge 25 carrying the Main lines at a higher level. Note the thick coating of soot showing how hard the colliery engines worked when bringing traffic from Oakes' Riddings Works and Colliery. The end of the platelayer's hut is seen on the right.
c.1904, Courtesy British Rail

Fig. 175
This view, facing Pinxton from near the signal box, shows the goods yard, shed, and loading dock adjoining the Down platform.
Just leaving for Nottingham Victoria is the 6.56spm from Pinxton hauled by LNER class L1 2-6-4 Tank 67753. Note the horizontal point rod compensator, centre foreground.
June 1960,
R W Sheppard

Fig. 176
This is a close view of the Station Master on the Up side beside the buildings of the later station. The booking office was on the left. The first station, opened two years after Pinxton, did not have the usual type of timber buildings seen on most of the Derbyshire Extension line.
June 1940, H H Mather

Fig. 177
A detailed shot of the brick warehouse and office with covered platform for loading the wagons. The signals and line on the right are Midland Railway.

June 1963, C A Evans

Fig. 178
The other side of this building also had a roof over the loading area.

June 1963, C A Evans

Fig. 179

Fig. 180
Facing north towards Pinxton along the Down platform, here is an excellent view of the station in wintry conditions. Although the land to the left of the scene drops quickly to the level of the river the height of the hillside into which the railway was cut shows clearly and includes the approach to the Up platform from the road. The buildings seen include the booking and Station Master's offices, but do not resemble the original Derbyshire Extension type. The station nameboard has early raised metal letters which read Pye Hill and Somercotes, and the original gas lamps.

1941, Mrs Janet Warsop,
David Hall collection

Fig. 181
This is an embracing shot of the station again looking north. On the left is the goods shed with an unusual mobile crane and a small platform beside the short siding. Further along, left of the first lamp post is the gable end of the weighbridge office. Beyond the small attractive flower beds is the Down side waiting room building with the 141 1/4 milepost on the left. The main buildings on the Up side are seen in more detail in Fig .

c.1938,
Mrs Janet Warsop,
David Hall collection

Fig. 182
This is a view of the south face of bridge 26, immediately north of Pye Hill station. It carries the earlier turnpike road (now B600) from Selston (right) to Somercotes and Alfreton (left). Just behind the new brick bridge, rebuilt in 1907 with additional brickwork to compensate for colliery subsidence, is the original timber structure. Beyond that again is an occupation bridge 27. The signals are a good example of the somersault arms used by the GNR. No.23 is Pye Hill's Down starter, beneath which is Palmerston Junction's Down Distant, painted red and white. Close by is the Fogsignalman's hut for use when needed at the Distant signal.

c.1907, Courtesy British Rail

Fig. 183
A view across the MR lines at Pye Bridge, near Riddings Junction, showing the connections into Pye Hill Colliery beneath the GNR Oakes' viaduct 24. The low clearance beneath here can be easily seen from the LNER class L1 2-6-4 tank crossing with the afternoon Nottingham-Pinxton train. The difference between Midland Railway lower quadrant semaphore signals and the GNR somersault arms seen on other photographs can be appreciated. Note the balance weight between the tracks to assist in pulling the distant signals off from Pye Bridge Junction, north of the station. The left hand arm signalled the Mansfield branch, and the right hand one indicated the route to Clay Cross and Chesterfield.

June 1960, A G Cramp

Fig. 184
The 0-4-0 saddle tank loco *Beaumont*, in immaculate condition, standing in the colliery yard at Pye Hill. The short wheelbase was necessary to negotiate the sharp curves near Oakes' viaduct, and the low height of the cab and boiler mountings, to pass beneath the Midland Railway's Erewash Valley lines. In the background can be seen the embankment and signal post on the GNR lines.

August 1954, John R Bonser

Fig. 185
Another view inside Pye Hill Colliery yard showing a different type of engine with the same restricted wheelbase and height as in Fig.171 p74. The scale of the cab height can be compared with the driver on the footplate here.

August 1954, John R Bonser

PALMERSTON JUNCTION
141 m 68 1/4 ch

After opening on 23rd August 1875, this became a busy junction drawing large quantities of coal from the Sleights and the early Pinxton Nos 1, 2 and 3 Collieries. Around the turn of the century deeper pits were sunk at Brookhill and Langton which gradually replaced the earlier Pinxton collieries. The Pinxton Colliery Company extended their network eastwards up the valley as the deeper pits were being sunk. In 1905 the GNR built a new branch from the south of Pinxton station to connect with the Colliery Company's extensions at Wharf Lane Junction. This resulted in coal traffic gradually dwindling away from Palmerston Junction. The junction and signal box remained *in situ*, but used unofficially by colliery wagons at times until around 1929. The installation was removed around 1947.

Fig. 186 (Top Right)
Bridge No.3 on the Palmerston branch carrying the GNR line to the empties sidings over the colliery lines
c.1907, Courtesy British Rail

Fig. 187
Bridge 1 on the short branch from Palmerston Junction to the early Pinxton Collieries, spanning the River Erewash, facing west. Note the iron-railed parapet, affording a good view of the varied eight- and ten-ton wagons loaded with coal, and the usual cast-iron notice warning against trespass on the left.
c. 1907, Courtesy British Rail

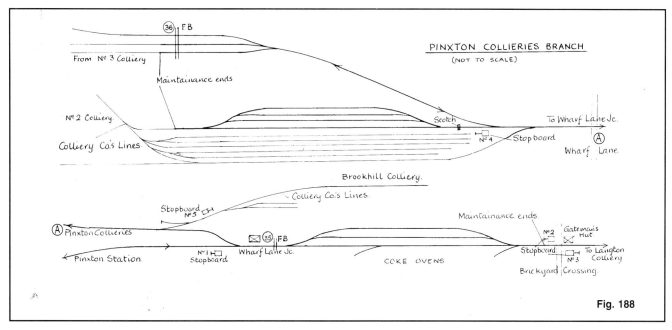

Fig. 188

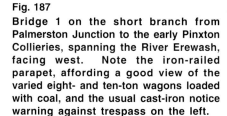

PINXTON 142 m 45 1/4 ch

For the construction of this station and the branch between 1873 and 1875, a double line junction named Langton Junction was built from the Midland Railway's Mansfield line (originally the Mansfield & Pinxton Railway laid as a tramway to the arm of the Cromford Canal at Pinxton Wharf) facing west towards Pye Bridge. This connection was severed and lifted after the opening of the station on 23rd August 1875 for goods and mineral traffic. Passenger services began on 1st August 1876.

The station buildings, which included the Station Master's house, were of a standard design for the Derbyshire Extension, and on the Down side arrival platform. The Up side departure platform was staggered, of island type, but had no shelters and was reached by a sleeper crossing. The usual goods shed was not built here, but a small brick building with sliding doors on opposite sides was situated near the dock. It was called the transit shed, and was used for holding traffic for and from the road van on the pick-up goods, and loading delivery items to the dray for local distribution.

The first passenger trains were worked by tank engines, chimney-first from Nottingham London Road. However a fatal accident occurred with a driver travelling bunker first, resulting in the subsequent installation of a turntable, a two-road engine shed and coaling stage. The engine shed did not last after the first World War, but the turntable remained in use to the end, together with the remnants of the coal stage, whose stocks provided a useful supplement

for the cottagers close by! Many colliers travelled to work on the first train to arrive in the morning, returning in the afternoon on an unadvertised service or Paddy train. A separate wooden waiting room was provided for these men near the entrance to the station.

The early collieries, Pinxton numbers 1, 2 and 3 were reached by a branch line from Palmerston Junction, a little over half a mile south of the station, but by the turn of the century deeper mines were sunk further up the valley at Langton, Brookhill and Bentinck, connected to the original ones by the colliery company's own lines.

To gain access to the new pits and coke ovens a new single line branch was constructed in 1905, leaving the Main lines opposite to the locomotive shed. The original signal box near both platform ends was replaced by a new one beyond the end of the departure platform. The branch climbed behind this new signal box and curved round to cross the Midland Railway by bridge 33 at approximately the site of Langton Junction. Crossing the adjacent River Erewash, it joined the colliery lines at Wharf Lane Junction, where two sidings and a run-round road were maintained as far as Brickyard Crossing. The GNR also upgraded and maintained the running road to the old collieries over Wharf Lane Crossing to sidings at numbers 2 and 3 pits. The working of empties to these pits was a hazardous operation in bad weather, for the engine ran round the train after arrival at Wharf Lane Junction, and after permission from a shunter at Wharf Lane Crossing, the train was propelled along the line to the sidings, some half a mile away.

Fig. 189
View facing east from the footbridge at Wharf Lane Junction on the 1905 colliery branch, showing the new Brookhill Colliery on the left; three GNR sidings centre, with an Ivatt class LI (LNER RI) 0-8-2 tank on the run round road, and the new coke oven plant right.

c.1910, Notts County Library

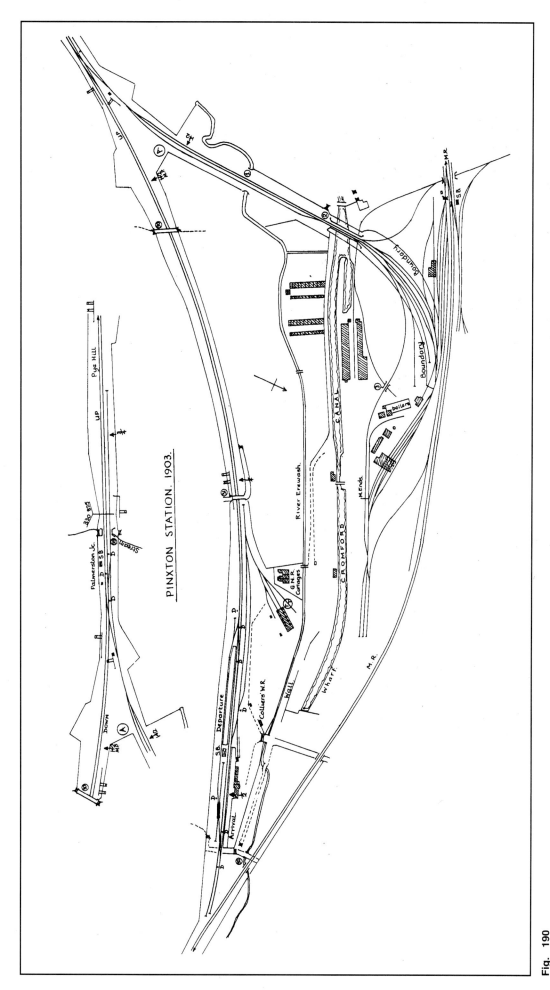

PINXTON STATION. 1903.

Fig. 190
Here was a hive of industry based on coal mining which had grown up around the wharf at the end of an arm from the Cromford Canal, originally fed by tramways including the Mansfield & Pinxton, opened in 1819. This was later bought by the Midland Railway, which had reached Codnor Park by 1847. The Mansfield & Pinxton line was widened to standard gauge 4 ft 8 1/2 in, realigned in places, and the Erewash Valley line extended from Codnor Park to join it in 1848. Until 1905 access to the Pinxton Collieries was from Palmerston Junction, almost threequarters of a mile south of the station. Occasionally, urgent traffic such as livestock was worked over this branch between the GN and GCR station at Kirkby and Pinxton (later Kirkby Bentinck). The Pinxton Colliery Company claimed a haulage charge when making sidings rebate applications to either company. The Pinxton Collieries branch was worked by a train staff kept at the station signal box. The station name appeared in the 1912 Handbook as Pinxton Wharf, and was renamed by British Railways in 1950 Pinxton South. It was closed to all traffic on 7th January 1963. No traces of this station remain today, except the three railway cottages opposite the Boat Inn by the side of the canal, which has a little water in it at this stretch. The area near the site of Palmerston Junction has a sewage filtration plant which discharges water into the River Erewash near to the vehicle scrapyard on the site of the collieries and their cottages.

Fig. 191
Footbridge 35 facing west from Wharf Lane. The MR wagons beyond the bridge are from Brookhill Colliery to the right. This bridge was erected in 1905 when the new branch was built to Langton Colliery.

c.1906, Courtesy British Rail

Fig. 192
The station approach looking east. In the foreground is bridge 32 across the River Erewash with a cast-iron lamp post to the right. The main buildings are of standard design for most of the Derbyshire Extension, the single storey section housing the Booking Hall, Waiting Room and Toilets; the two-storey section being the Station Master's residence, with the booking/parcels office beneath the first bedroom. A brick wall across to the fencing ensured privacy of this part. The brick building to the right with a loading stage and sliding doors on both sides was a transit shed, where traffic for delivery by dray or lorry was unloaded from wagon or van on the other side. Traffic for dispatch was kept here, and loaded into the road van for Nottingham or Manchester Deansgate. Likewise consignments of flour, tea-chests, and consumer goods were unloaded from rail to be kept until delivered by road to local merchants. There was no Goods shed/Warehouse.

April 1962, L Little

Fig. 193
The short dock and loading gauge seen from the end of the departure platform. Opposite the loading gauge is a sleeper-built coal bunker, and to the right, a van body used as the depot for storage of Earle's Cement.

April 1962, L Little

Fig. 194
A good view of the station from the embankment of the colliery branch line showing LNER class L1 tank 67741 having arrived with a train from Nottingham Victoria. The original corbels on the Station House chimneys have been removed, and the goods yard sidings are full of wagons being stored prior to breaking up. Away to the right is a northbound empties train on the Midland Railway lines.

April 1962, J Cupit

Fig. 195
This view of the signal box, renamed Pinxton South Station by BR in 1950, shows the Main lines running south to be joined beyond the crossover by the 1905 colliery branch. Bridge 31 which stood behind the signals was removed in September 1924. The two disc signals near the signal box (17 and 25, Fig.203 p86) are of standard LNER-type. Signal arm 5 has been removed from the bracket on the left, the branch being no longer in use.

June 1962, A Henshaw

Fig. 196
There was once an engine shed at Pinxton, but it did not survive after world war I.   This view of LNER class E1 2-4-0 704 taking water after turning shows part of the building with the ash pit road in the foreground. With the building and operation of the Coke Ovens, and collieries further up the valley, the River Erewash became very polluted and the water drawn up here was so dirty that some drivers would rather take water at Eastwood. *April 1912, F Gillford*

Fig. 197
A detailed shot of the turntable, little used in the latter years, as the passenger trains were usually worked by tank engines. The handle left of the notice on the far side worked the bolt for securing the table in position. The right-hand one was used to push the table round. *June 1962, A Henshaw*

Fig. 198
This view of the arrival platform and main buildings of the standard design for most stations along the Derbyshire Extension lines, is taken from the end of the departure platform, and includes the sleeper crossing which connected the two platforms. LNER class J 39 0-6-0 loco 64974, fitted with an ex-NER type tender, has just run round the train after arrival. Note the four fire-buckets hanging beneath the station nameboard, the GNR-type lamp posts, originally gas lit, and the extra coaches on the left. Beyond the coaches at the platform is bridge 33 which carried the colliery branch over the Midland Railway. The coke oven plant chimneys show above the coaches in the departure platform line.
October 1955, John R Bonser

Fig. 199
The view approaching the terminus with the signal box right, behind which the 1905 branch to the later collieries climbs to cross the Midland Railway's lines to Kirkby and Mansfield. The 6.56pm passenger train to Nottingham stands in the station with Brookhill Colliery in the distance.
June 1962, A Henshaw

Fig. 200
Just one side of the departure platform is in use by now. The LNER Class J39 64974 has shunted its four coaches onto those already stabled, and appears prepared to leave tender first rather than use the turntable and run forwards. The staggered platforms show up well here together with the wagon and van standing in the Dock beside the cement store on the left.
October 1955, John R Bonser

Fig. 201
The view from the coke ovens, looking west along the new branch from Pinxton Station, and the GNR-maintained branch to Wharf Lane crossing and the earlier pits to the right. The new wooden footbridge 35 was later replaced and extended to cross the numerous sidings at Brookhill Colliery.
c.1907, Courtesy British Rail

Fig. 202
Facing south at bridge 31 before reaching the station. On the left is the Up starter and Palmerston Junction Up distant with the early type red colouring. On the right is the buffer stop at the end of the shunt from the turntable and coal stage. The milepost just beyond the bridge is 124 1/2 miles from King's Cross.
c.1907, Courtesy British Rail

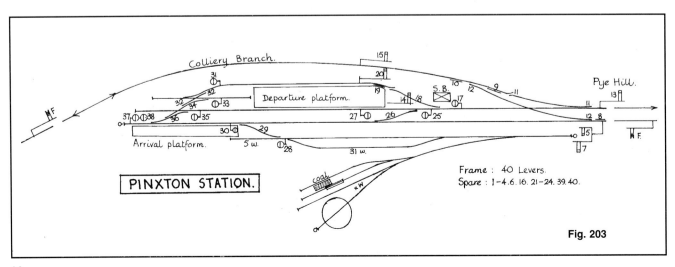

PINXTON STATION.

Colliery Branch.

Departure platform.

Arrival platform.

Pye Hill.

coal

Frame : 40 Levers.
Spare : 1-4. 6. 16. 21-24. 39. 40.

Fig. 203

Fig. 204
The Pinxton Collieries engine shed at Brookhill, showing six-coupled tank engine *Emfour 2* outside, and a similar type inside the shed. Note the oil cans above the left-hand buffer. This engine was built by Hudswell Clarke of Leeds in 1954 (works no 1877). It was one of four for the NCB East Midlands No 4 Area and was sent new to Pinxton No 2 shed and transferred to Brookhill shed in 1955.
March 1956, John R Bonser

Fig. 205
A close-up shot of Peckett No.2 0-4-0 Saddle tank just outside the engine shed. Works no 1975, built in 1939 and sent to Pinxton Collieries Ltd, it was withdrawn in 1959. The large heads of the buffers show up well; they were necessary to avoid buffers locking when negotiating the sharp curves in the yard during shunting operations.
March 1956, John R Bonser

Fig. 206
A close-up of the 1905 bridge 33 seen from the Midland Railway, facing west, with a Down train approaching Sleights East Signal box.
c.1906, Courtesy British Rail

4. AWSWORTH STATION - ILKESTON

AWSWORTH 135m 35ch

An unusual, small station, which was built shortly after the opening of the line to Egginton Junction, and was opened for both goods and passenger traffic on 1st November 1880. The platforms were opposite each other, with a level crossing at the eastern end used by passengers, there being no footbridge. The crossing served an unmetalled occupation road to Shilo, where the colliery was, but it was little used between the wars, and the gates were not operated from the signal box, but padlocked, and operated by the porter on duty from his hut. The wicket gates for pedestrians were locked by levers 29 and 30 in the signal box.

The platform buildings were all of timber construction with slate roofs, there being booking facilities on the Down side. Nearer the western end of the Down platform was a cast iron urinal similar to the one at Kimberley. The Station Master's house was a detached blue brick building standing close to the crossing gates on the Up side.

Awsworth Colliery, situated on the north side of the running lines at Shilo, was already served by the Nottingham Canal and the Midland Railway's mineral branch from Bennerley Sidings, and the GNR laid two sidings on the Up side from which a short branch served it. The colliery had ceased production by 1898. However, beside the River Erewash to the west, the Awsworth Colliery Company built the Bennerley Ironworks with three blast furnaces. This was served by a single-line branch which dropped steeply to the valley floor beside the Main lines, and needed two bridges to cross a minor road and the Nottingham Canal. The latter was a timber trestle viaduct. Engines working this branch had to face Awsworth chimney first. The ironworks ceased production by 1934 because of the collapse of two furnaces which were being re-lined. With the retirement of the last stationmaster, Mr Eames, the same year, the branch was closed and lifted. Station working then transferred to Kimberley. The acceptance of goods traffic, latterly a wagon or two of coal left at the entrance to the sidings for the local Co-operative Society, ceased on 1st August 1943. The signal box was closed, sidings and points recovered in May 1954, the Up starting signal, number 24 becoming an outer home for Awsworth Junction. Beyond bridge 51, it is possible to walk along the grass-covered track bed as far as the station; alternatively the road past Barlow's Cottages offers an easier route. From here, the public footpath follows the track bed, and divides to follow either the Main line at bridge 53 or the Bennerley branch line to bridge 1; both bridges have now been removed. At the time of writing (1999) the footpath does not continue to the Bennerley Viaduct, but a short walk along the road leads to the Nottingham Canal. To the east the canal has been filled in, but Naphtha House (see Fig.216 p91) can be seen. To the west the canal is now a fishing amenity, and the footpath continues beside the canal. To the north of the railway, as far as the Awsworth bypass, the ground has been levelled to create a recreation area.

Fig. 207
A Nottingham-Derby Friargate passenger train headed by BR standard 2MT class loco 43061 rolls down the gradient into the station, which is neatly kept. The earlier nameboard has been replaced by BR enamelled smaller version on the lamp-post, but there is no signal box at the end of the Up platform. Part of the Station House is seen on the left.

August 1963, A G Cramp

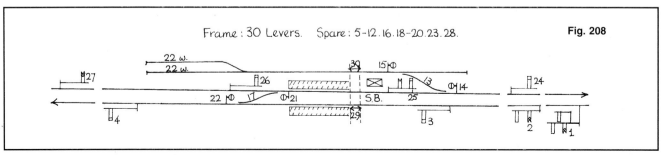

Frame: 30 Levers.   Spare: 5-12.16.18-20.23.28.

Fig. 208

Fig. 209
This view of the station is taken from the Down platform facing east. On the Up platform is the modest shelter/waiting room beyond which stands the Station House and signalbox. The head shunt buffer stops can be seen right of the signal post, but the porter is more interested in the photographer.
Pre 1923, Andrew Knighton Collection

Fig. 210
The south face of bridge 51 over Awsworth Lane, east of the station; beyond is seen part of the Giltbrook viaduct on the Pinxton branch, with 'The Gate Inn' between. Built on the 'skew' of limestone pillars and abutments from the Kimberley cutting, it is some 50 ft above the road.
c.1910, Courtesy British Rail

Fig. 211
Bridge 54, carrying the Main lines over the Nottingham Canal at Awsworth. Bridge 2 on the Bennerley branch is seen beyond. On the right can be seen wagons in one of the two sidings beside the Up Main line.
c.1910, Courtesy British Rail

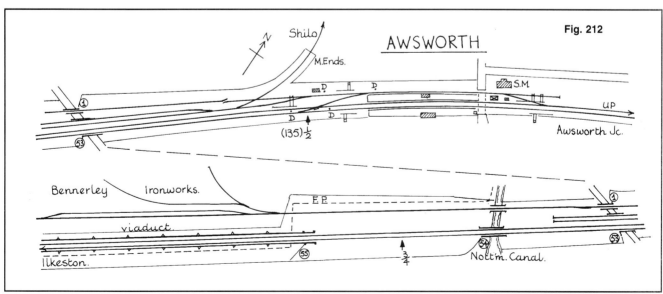

THE ILKESTON (BENNERLEY) VIADUCT
135m 63ch to 136m 4ch.

Built between 1876 and 1877, this slender wrought iron structure ranks as the second largest undertaking on the Derbyshire Extension. It spans a wide part of the Erewash Valley prone to mining subsidence and of soft soils. The abutments and pillars for the spans across the Midland Railway's lines at the western end were of brick and faced with blue bricks. The foundations were of concrete faced with blue bricks. The trestle piers were made up of segmented wrought iron columns linked together with pin-jointed bracing. Instead of the usual four longitudinal girders beneath the tracks, three only, were used and these too were of lattice wrought iron construction for lightness and affording less wind resistance. Trough decking extended across these main girders. All the ironwork was prefabricated and assembled on site, making the construction rapid and replacements or spares a simple matter. Estimated total weight of the viaduct on the foundations was only 12 cwt per square foot! The original handrails along its length were replaced with a lattice parapet shortly after its opening. Now a Grade II listed building it is the only remaining one of five to have been constructed to a similar design. Another one at Meldon, still extant, has a steel deck with a road along it.

A Trust has been formed to renovate, preserve and use the viaduct, possibly as a cycle/walkway along the disused railway route, but embankments at either end have been removed, and nothing more than plans are certain in 1999.

The site of Bennerley Ironworks is now occupied by a large opencast coal plant for collecting, blending and loading the coal from surrounding sites to rail for despatch to power stations. The rapid loading bunker which stands beside the viaduct holds 2,000 tons of blended coal and is fitted with automatic vehicle identification computerised for feeding information to TOPS (Total Operations Processing System) or customers. It has been mothballed since 1994.

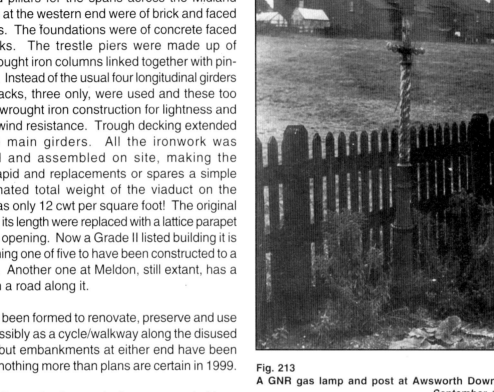

Fig. 213
A GNR gas lamp and post at Awsworth Down platform.
September 1964, A Henshaw

Fig. 214
High embankments, bridges and viaducts were needed to cross the Erewash valley to reach Ilkeston. This view from beside the Nottingham Canal shows the western abutment of bridge 54, now strengthened with brickwork over the original limestone, a short embankment, and the wrought iron Bennerley Viaduct being crossed by a mineral empties train for Colwick. Along the foot of the embankment can be seen the line of the Bennerley branch. The wooden viaduct over the canal was removed in the 1930s.
August 1960, A Henshaw

Fig. 215
Seen from the hill on which Awsworth is situated the whole of the south side of the Bennerley viaduct is visable together with the chimney of the ironworks boiler house. The line of the Nottingham canal is crossing the foreground and beyond the viaduct is the village of Cotmanhay.

An unidentified loco is working an east coast special across the viaduct which changes from the wrought iron structure to steel plate girders on brick columns to cross the MR Erewash valley lines.

August 1960, A. Henshaw

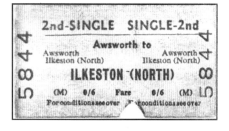

Fig. 216
Another view of bridges 1 and 53 beyond, from the north side. The road beneath led from Bennerley Ironworks over the Nottingham canal beside Naphtha House (which is behind the photographer) to Awsworth.

c.1910, Courtesy British Rail

Fig. 217
A view along the Bennerley branch facing Awsworth Station showing bridge 1 on the branch, and bridge 53 (right) on the Main lines. The Station Master's house is right of the tree. At this time traffic was still worked out of Bennerley Ironworks.

February 1928, B Beer collection

Fig. 218

Fig. 219

Fig. 220

Detail of one column of the viaduct and its blue brick/concrete base. There were longitudinal girders borne on the columns. Note the drain pipe from the channel beside the track. Midland men referred to this viaduct as the 'nuts & bolts' viaduct, but where it was not rivetted the braces were secured with cotter pins, as Fig. 220 shows.

March 1974, A Henshaw

Fig. 221
Detail of the three main lattice girders at the top of a column. Notice the three plank catwalk along each side for inspection purposes. Access to this was obtained by a trap door and steps at each end of the viaduct.
March 1974, A Henshaw

Fig. 222
This view, facing north along the Erewash Canal beside Stenson's Lock and cottage shows an unidentified re-boilered LNER class O4 hauling a train of mineral empties from Stanton to Colwick crossing bridge 56. The canal is maintained and navigable, but the bridge, embankments and lock-keeper's cottage have gone.
August 1961, A Henshaw

Fig. 223
The view along the Erewash Canal, looking north from Stenson's Lock at Bennerley, to compare with Fig.222. Gone are the lock-keeper's cottage, the GNR bridge 56, and the embankment west of the canal. The short embankment leading to the viaduct is seen right , well covered with hawthorn and bramble. The tower of Eastwood church can now be seen on the horizon above the canal.
April 1992, A Henshaw

Fig. 224
A view of the viaduct to compare with Fig.214 p90 . It was taken from the filled-in part of the Nottingham Canal north of the GNR line and shows the fenced footpath leading left to where the canal has water in its bed, south of the line. The embankment between bridge 54 and the viaduct has been removed to provide a visual/sound barrier between the footpath and the opencast coal disposal plant in the distance, which is standing at the western end of the viaduct.
August 1987, A Henshaw

ILKESTON 136 m 70 1/2 ch

Service began for passengers on 4th April 1878 and goods on 10th January 1878. On opening the passenger station was built to the standard design adopted on the Derbyshire Extension, with slate roofed buildings on the Up side and red brick combined buildings on the Down side. The opposite platforms were connected by a latticed ironwork foot overbridge. The East signal box opened on 27th July 1891, after the opening of the Heanor branch on 1st July 1891 when a bay platform was installed at the west end of the Down platform. Passenger trains for Heanor left from the bay platform and trains arriving from the Heanor branch used the north side of the Up island platform. Coal traffic became so heavy by 1904 that serious delays were being encountered on the Up Main at Stanton Junction and to alleviate the position, on Sunday 1st May that year, the Heanor passenger line running alongside the Up Main Stanton Junction to Ilkeston was made a slow running line for goods and coal traffic under the Permissive Block system. Stanton Junction then turned passenger trains from the Heanor branch to the Up Main for discharging at Ilkeston. The Up shunt siding at Ilkeston.West was then used as a stabling siding.

Various alterations took place in 1914 following increases in both passenger and freight traffic. The waiting accommodation on the Up island platform was improved and a timber roof supported on iron brackets was built to cover both sides of the platform. Red brick buildings comprising booking hall, booking and parcels offices were built fronting the Heanor Road which crossed the line at the east end of the station on a brick and iron girder bridge (62). The frontage of the building was 70 ft with a working depth of 40 ft. The latticed ironwork passenger overbridge was replaced by a corrugated-iron covered red brick and girder footway leading from the new booking hall, with similarly covered stone staircases leading down to the platforms. A clerestory timber roof supported on iron columns was installed to cover the Down platform for the entire length of the combined buildings and dwelling house. The part alongsde the house was demolished some years later because it made the living room so dark. The booking hall on the Down side platform became a gentlemen's waiting room; the booking office the Station Master's office, and the parcels office the general waiting room. Some years after the First World War the old booking hall reverted to the general waiting room and the old parcels office then became a class room for the station ambulance team. On the freight side additions were made to the Stanton Junction and West Yards, and a turntable installed in the West Yard. Colliery engines were permitted to turn on this table for 2/6d (12.5p) a time, payable in cash before departure.

Along the south side of the Heanor passenger bay platform was a nursery garden with a large greenhouse and here were raised the shrubs and plants for the station gardens of the Nottinghamshire and Derbyshire area of the Great Northern. At the west end of the nursery stood the water pumping house with a stationary steam engine pumping water from a deep well to an overhead storage tank to supply the parachute water cranes at both ends of the passenger station as well as one in Stanton Junction yard and one at Nutbrook Junction.

The Stanton Junction yard was the marshalling point for ironstone and other traffic for the Stanton branch and Ironworks. The Up side west yard was for the collection and marshalling of coal traffic from the eight nearby collieries and the iron products from the Stanton Ironworks. The Manners Colliery branch originally led off the west yard but after the opening of the Heanor branch the connection was transferred to Nutbrook Junction, and the two lines leading from the west yard were buffer stopped at the east end to become the GN Manners Colliery Empty Sidings.

The large goods depot which was on the east side of bridge 62 had road access from both the Cotmanhay and Heanor Roads The red brick goods shed had an upper storey warehouse with two grain hoists originally worked by horses but converted to electric motor in the 1940s. The shed deck had a 30-cwt crane and the yard a 10-ton crane. Situated at the Cotmanhay Road entrance were stables, motor garage, work and paint shops of the District Engineer's Department. Opposite the garage and stables was a concrete-built combined office and cement store,

Fig. 225
A view from beside the station bridge 62 facing east shows a a WD 2-8-0 (Austerity) pulling a Down train past Ilkeston East signal box, and the goods yard (right).
c.1960, D Webb

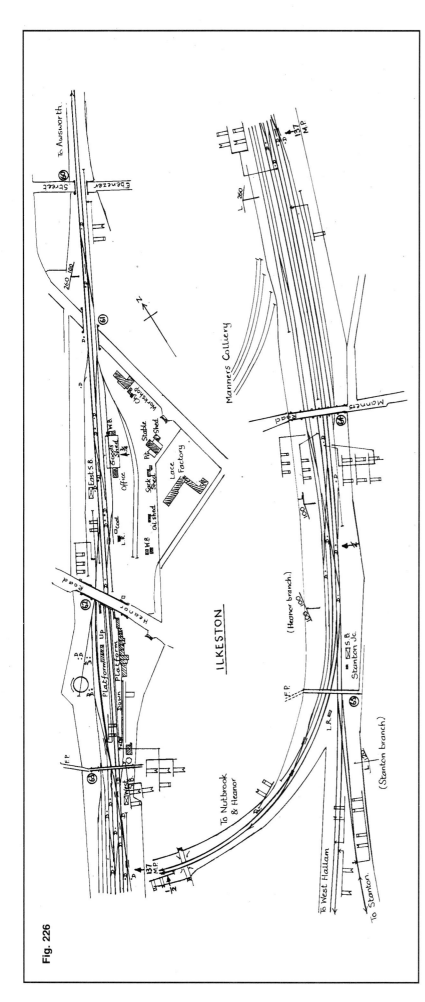

Fig. 226

ILKESTON

To Ausworth.

Ebenezer Street

Manners Colliery

To Nutbrook & Heanor

To West Hallam

To Stanton.

(Heanor branch.)

(Stanton branch.)

137 M.P.

Stanton Jc.

erected and used by the Barnstone Cement Company in the 1930s furnished with a coal-fired boiler and central heating system. The Anglo American Oil Company had a siding in the goods yard to deal with tank wagons. A red brick built office and weighbridge for road vehicles was situated at the Heanor Road entrance. The Down refuge siding held 21 wagons, engine and van, and the Up refuge siding 31 wagons, engine and van. This was extended to join the turntable road with a double slip connection. Ilkeston East signal box controlled the goods yard working. Sidings coming under the supervision of Ilkeston station were Manners, Ilkeston Dale, Woodside, Coppice and Nutbrook Collieries, Oakwell Brick and Tile Works, Derby Road Goods Depot and the Stanton Ironworks sidings of Hallam Fields, New Works and Dale Pipe Works.

The station was renamed Ilkeston North on 1st July

1950. The Sunday passenger service was withdrawn on 11th November 1962, and all passenger services ceased on 7th September 1964. The final closure date was 27th May 1968.

The goods yard site is now occupied with a modern single-storey factory building which replaces the old warehouse, and the bridges 59 to 61 over streets in Cotmanhay dismantled. Gone too are the weighbridge and office by the entrance gate to the Derby road depot, together with the goods shed and coal merchants' Stack yard which are occupied by extensions of the adjacent garage/car sales business. A modern police station now occupies the site of the station buildings fronting the Heanor road. The rest of the station site, as far as Stanton Junction has been partially filled in and is covered with vegetation. At Stanton Junction, the Manners Industrial Site has been built, with numerous

factories. The Stanton Branch is now a footpath as far as West end drive, with footbridge 3 (seen in Figs.289 & 290 p119 & 120) removed. Gone too are the weighbridge and office by the entrance gate to the Derby Road Depot, together with the Goods shed and coal merchants' Stack yard, which are occupied by extensions of the adjacent garage/car sales business.

The Pewit golf course has been extended across the trackbed, but there is a footpath across grassland to the GN main Line trackbed and the MR Shipley branch beside the Nut Brook. From here are bridle roads and tracks to Manners Industrial Site and Shipley Park. The trackbed south of Derby Road as far as Bridge 8 at Little Hallam is walkable with difficulty, and the remains of two brickkilns at Oakwell, although Listed Buildings, are quite decrepit and surrounded with vegetation.

Fig. 227
A sparkling 0-8-2T 137 arrives at Ilkeston with the 2.43pm miners' train from Gedling to West Hallam. (Note the platelayers working on the Down Main). These engines were designed by H A Ivatt for the London suburban services, but proved too heavy and damaged the track with their rapid acceleration. After a while they were transferred to Colwick and the West Riding for colliery workings, but again proved troublesome because of the small capacity of their tanks.
May 1912, the late H F Gillford

Fig. 228
This early picture of the station, looking east, is taken from the Up platform, and shows clearly the main buildings and Stationmaster's House on the opposite side, and conforming to the standard pattern. The additional building nearer the bridge would be for porters and other staff such as shunters, one of whom can be seen with his shunting pole on the right, for the room between the urinals and ladies waiting room was used as the Station Master's office. The lattice girder footbridge connecting the platforms was later boxed in when extensions were made. The Heanor road crosses by bridge 62, immediately behind this footbridge. Note the angled nameboards on each platform, an unusual feature, beneath which is a notice 'Change for Marlpool and Heanor'. Beyond the nameboard on the left is a cast iron urinal which was removed in 1940, with those at Awsworth and Kimberley, to assist the war effort.
c.1910, Author's Collection

Fig. 229
The goods shed, east end, facing the station bridge 62 with the East signal box (right).
June 1966, A Henshaw

Fig. 230
The rear of the goods shed, then used as the area distribution parcels depot, showing awning over the loading docks.
June 1966, A Henshaw

Fig. 231
The weighbridge and office near the exit to the goods yard. This was typical of those along the Derbyshire Extension.
June 1966, A Henshaw

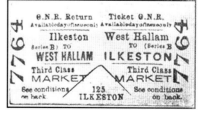

Fig. 232
Another view facing east from the road bridge 64 leading to Manners Colliery shows more of the track layout and the West signal box. The footbridge 63 is in the middle distance. The pumphouse is prominent behind the signal box.
c.1947, H C Whitelock

Fig. 234
The exterior of the station buildings from the Heanor Road showing the extensions built in 1924, and the original platform buildings behind the wooden gate. A police station now occupies this site.
February 1956, P Stevenson

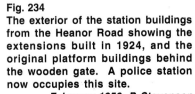

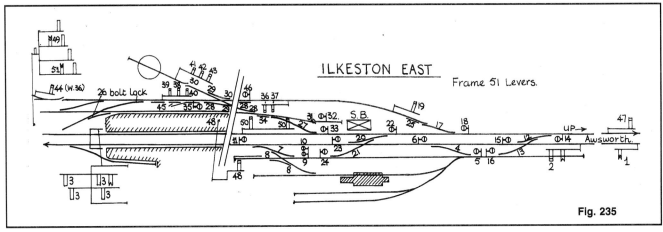

ILKESTON EAST

Frame 51 Levers.

Fig. 235

Fig. 236
Ilkeston Station seen from the footbridge (62A) above the Main lines facing west. Although the Station House and platform buildings were built to standard pattern, they were extended to include first class waiting room and extra toilets later. The Down side buildings were not of the standard wooden design. The building beyond the Up platform (left) is the pumphouse. Beyond that, beneath the lattice footbridge, is the West signal box with its gantry of repeating Home signals.
July 1954, G A Yeomans

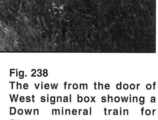

Fig. 237
This view of the station from the embankment beside bridge 62 shows the Up side island platform and the covered footbridge and stairway. Heanor trains would normally arrive at the nearest platform, the departure signal 48 for which is beside the stairway. The brick waiting room can be seen right of the awning with the pumphouse further right. The bridge plate 62A is visible on the brickwork left of the signal post.
c.1964, P Smith

Fig. 238
The view from the door of West signal box showing a Down mineral train for Stanton passing the home signals, almost obscured by steam. There are coaches in the Heanor bay between the departure signal 46 and the pumphouse.
c.1947, H C Whitelock

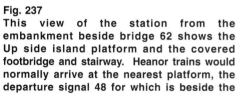

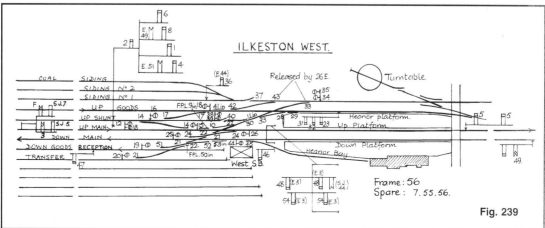

Fig. 239

Fig. 240
The station, facing east from the end of the Down platform. The difference between the Down side buildings and the standard wooden ones is obvious with part of the awning removed. The Heanor bay is now full of weeds, there being no West box working. To the right of the platform, the buildings are the extended parcels/booking offices.   *c.1964, P Smith*

Fig. 241
An unusual disc signal raised some 8ft above the ground to make it visible above the parapet of Bridge 61 to drivers about to set back into the Down departure from the Main line. The signals beside the Up Main are East's Home No.2, and West's Up distant.   *September 1964, A Henshaw*

Fig. 242
The young signalman himself poses at the west end of his signal box. After working many of the GNR boxes in this area, Cecil became a relief signalman and was transferred to the ex-Midland Erewash Valley lines after closure of the Derbyshire Extension lines, eventually becoming an Inspector at Derby LM Region.   *c.1948, H C Whitelock*

Fig. 243
The unusual interior of Ilkeston North Station signal box , formerly Ilkeston East, showing two contrasting types of lever frame. On the right is the Saxby and Farmer rocker frame installed when this box was rebuilt in 1907, to replace the one which was demolished by an engine on August 2nd of that year. On the left is an LMS tappet frame installed in November 1958 after the West signal box was gutted by fire, to enable Down side movements formerly controlled from there to be worked from the one box. The position of this frame and the shelf of block instruments severely restricts the signalman's movements, and cuts off the original fireplace with its brick flue.
November 1958, H H Mather collection

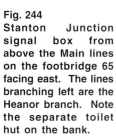

Fig. 244
Stanton Junction signal box from above the Main lines on the footbridge 65 facing east. The lines branching left are the Heanor branch. Note the separate toilet hut on the bank.
July 1954,
G A Yeomans

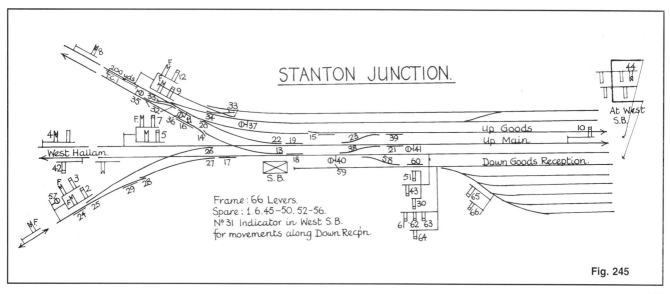

STANTON JUNCTION.

Frame : 66 Levers.
Spare : 1.6.45–50. 52–56.
Nº 31 Indicator in West S.B.
for movements along Down Recpn.

Fig. 245

Fig. 246
The Up and Down sidings between West signal box and Stanton Junction facing west. The site of the West signal box was beside the post (left) and behind the buffer stop above the bridge. The replacement ground frame is behind the lamp post.
September 1964, A Henshaw

Fig. 247
The view approaching Stanton Junction from between the Down goods reception line and the Main line shows the miniature somersault arms for shunting movements (left), and the three Home signals on the bracket. In the distance is footbridge 65.
1964, H H Mather

Fig. 248
The view along the Main lines from Derby, facing east from footbridge 65 near Stanton Junction, prior to closure. By now there were just a few trains to Derby, Egginton and Burton through the Stanton branch was used to the end. The removal of signals from the left hand post of the bracket signal indicates removal of the goods line from the Heanor branch. The fogman's hut with indicators stands between the Main lines and the Stanton branch which has a double-headed train of mineral empties for Colwick passing hauled by two Class 25 diesels. Footbridge 65 obscures the gable of the signal box beyond, and bridge 64 leading to Manners Colliery is visible above it.

April 1968, A G Cramp

Fig. 249 & Fig. 250
Fogman's indicators at Stanton Junction situated beside the hut; they were similar to those inside signal boxes to indicate whether a distant was off or on.
September 1964, A Henshaw

Fig. 251
Footbridge 65 seen from beside the Heanor branch showing Stanton Junction signal box beneath. Disc 37 right, beside the branch lines and sidings with wagons in is on the left.
c.1910,
Courtesy British Rail

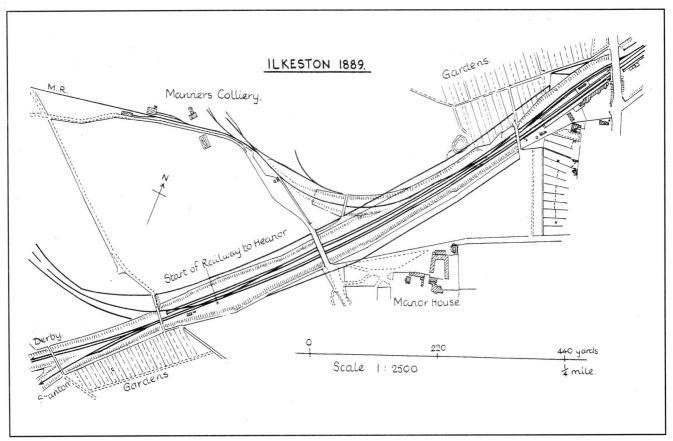

ILKESTON 1889.

M. R.

Manners Colliery.

Gardens.

N

Start of Railway to Heanor

Manor House.

Derby.

Stanton Gardens

0   220   440 yards
Scale 1:2500   ¼ mile.

Fig. 252 ILKESTON PLAN 1889
This is taken from a GNR plan presented to a Mr Latta, for construction of the Heanor Branch, which is shown by a single line marking the centre of the tracks diverging from just east of Stanton Junction signal box, together with additional land purchased for extensions at Ilkeston and for the branch itself. The new outer boundaries are marked thicker than the originals. Items of interest shown here are

(a) The first station buildings on the Down side which are of standard design (see Kimberley, Fig.61 p30 & Fig.67 p32).
(b) Awning around the Up side waiting rooms.
(c) The entrance to Manners Colliery from west of the station.
(d) More detail outside the boundary lines, and shading for the cuttings, which are not shown on the 1903-4 plans used throughout for the scale layout details.

5. NUTBROOK AND HEANOR BRANCH

This branch of 71 chains from Ilkeston West to Shipley Colliery was authorised by an Act of 1880, and opened on 7th June 1886. The route was constructed for a short distance to serve the adjacent Manners Colliery but abandoned after 1892 in favour of a branch from Stanton Junction to Heanor, authorised by an Act of 16th July 1885, for 3 1/2 miles as far as Shipley. The first section to be opened, on the 4th June 1886 was from Ilkeston West to Nutbrook, a distance of 1 mile, 22 chains. A further Act of 5th July 1887 authorised the branch to be extended from Shipley to Heanor with consequent alterations to Ilkeston passenger station and the erection of Ilkeston East signal box. Plans to extend the branch further still to serve collieries at Swanwick and reach Alfreton were drawn up but never implemented.

NUTBROOK JUNCTION 137 m 70 ch

A new branch to Manners Colliery was built from Nutbrook Junction and opened on 1st January 1892. It was controlled from Nutbrook Junction signal box, after which the original branch from Ilkeston West was disconnected. This Manners branch was worked by a series of stop boards controlled by the colliery staff, because the Midland Railway had access to the branch midway between Nutbrook Junction and the colliery. The facilities at the Junction consisted of a red brick built shunters' cabin and lamp room, parachute water tank, and timber-constructed coaling stage. The Great Northern sidings connected at the north end with the Shipley Colliery Company's network worked by their own steam engines serving the Nutbrook,

Woodside and Coppice collieries. The coaling stage was demolished in August 1960.

The single-line branch to Marlpool and Heanor stations was worked by train staff only. This was crescent-shaped, lettered on one side "Go on to Heanor" and on the other "Go on to Nutbrook". On 24th June 1904, the branch was divided into two sections, Nutbrook Junction to Marlpool, and Marlpool to Heanor. Nutbrook Junction held a circular shaped staff lettered "Nutbrook to Marlpool" one side and on the reverse "Marlpool to Nutbrook". Nutbrook Junction also held train tickets which were white, printed "Down Nutbrook to Marlpool" and red "Up Marlpool to Nutbrook". On the closing of Marlpool signal box the original crescent-shaped staff was used.

Fig. 253
A general view of Manners Colliery from above the empties sidings with one of their own wagons in the foreground. The footbridge leads to Manners Road, which crossed the GNR Main lines further left. The original connection to the colliery was *via* these sidings from Ilkeston West.

Courtesy Erewash Museum

Fig. 254
Although showing no details of track layout for the GNR here, the earlier lines of the Midland Railway to the Shipley collieries together with existing colliery lines are indicated. Bridge 3 spans the Midland Railway's Manners Colliery branch from Mapperley Junction. Bridge 4 carries a road over the branch at Nutbrook, and just north of this, the line to Nutbrook Colliery sidings leaves the Heanor Branch. The Nutbrook section contract terminated just south of the colliery sidings, and was opened for traffic before the line to Heanor was constructed beyond Nutbrook. Just beyond Nutbrook Colliery, a footbridge spanned the three colliery lines from Shipley collieries further north, and close by were two cottages. With the expansion of coal traffic before the 1914-18 war, the sidings at Nutbrook were extended northwards, necessitating the removal of the cottages, and an extension of the footbridge over the extra lines (Fig.257 p107).

Fig. 254

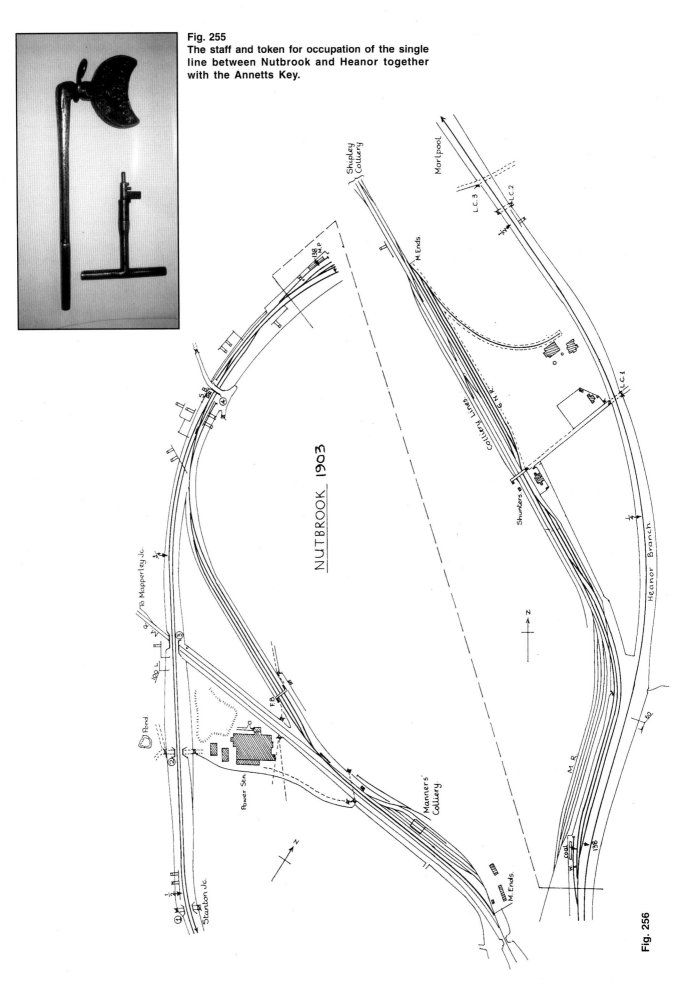

Fig. 255
The staff and token for occupation of the single line between Nutbrook and Heanor together with the Annetts Key.

NUTBROOK 1903

Fig. 256

Fig. 257
The footbridge over GN-maintained and colliery sidings at Nutbrook beyond the cottage seen in Fig.254 p105. The 1903 scale plan (Fig.256 p106) shows a pair of cottages on the site of the nearer span, beneath which the three GN sidings were continued after the demolition of the cottages before 1914. The bridge was reconstructed to cover the GN-maintained sidings in 1915.

March 1966, A Henshaw

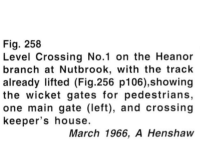

Fig. 258
Level Crossing No.1 on the Heanor branch at Nutbrook, with the track already lifted (Fig.256 p106),showing the wicket gates for pedestrians, one main gate (left), and crossing keeper's house.

March 1966, A Henshaw

Fig. 259
The water tower minus its leather sock was the only relic left at Nutbrook when this photograph was taken. The coaling stage was behind the photographer who was facing south towards Stanton Junction. Immediately under bridge 4 in the distance was the branch to Manners colliery.

July 1974, I D Stones

Fig. 260
Coal from Shipley, Coppice and Woodside Collieries was brought by privately owned locomotives along colliery lines to the sorting sidings at Nutbrook for collection by GNR or Midland locomotives. This picture shows the colliery weighbridge and office just north of the GNR maintained sidings (Fig.256 p106). Note the white signal left of the telegraph pole in the distance.

March 1966, A Henshaw

Fig. 261
By this time the GNR connection had been removed from the foreground leaving colliery lines and the MR connection behind the signal post.

March 1966, A. Henshaw

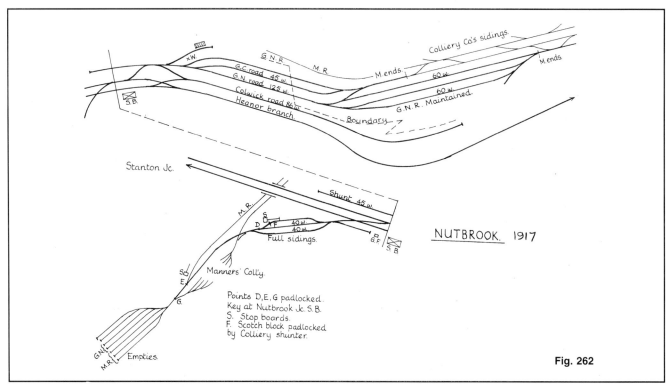

NUTBROOK. 1917

Stanton Jc.

Shunt 45 w.

Full sidings.

Manners' Coll'y.

Points D,E,G padlocked.
Key at Nutbrook Jc. S.B.
S. Stop boards.
F. Scotch block padlocked
by Colliery shunter.

G.N.R.
M.R.
Empties.

Colliery Co's sidings.
G.N.R.
M.R.
M.ends.
M.ends.
G.C. road 45 w.
G.N. road 125 w.
Colwick road 86 w.
Heanor branch.
60 w.
60 w.
G.N.R. Maintained.
Boundary.
S.B.
×W.

Fig. 262

MARLPOOL for SHIPLEY 139 m 51 1/4 ch

This small station was opened on 1st July 1891 for passenger and parcels traffic only. It had an island platform with well-designed brick buildings, situated in a cutting and was reached by a flight of steps from the footbridge 12. A passing loop here was controlled from the station signal box. During the construction of the line through Shipley Park a Roman urn was found containing coins from the reigns of several Roman emperors from Claudius AD 41 to Tacitus AD 276.

The station house was a detached building close to which was a row of cottages for railway staff, all built to a design approved by Squire Miller Mundy of Shipley Hall, for whose convenience the station was built. All the passenger trains stopped here.

Meynell's Coppice Crossing No 1 was 1 mile 17 chains from Nutbrook Junction and Heanor Coppice Crossing No 2 was 1 mile 2 1/2 chains north of Marlpool station. There were bridges over the branch at 138 miles 69 chains (No 8), which carried the private coach road to Shipley Hall, and at 139 miles 17 chains (No 9) which carried three colliery sidings to the adjacent Woodside Colliery. A lattice girder footbridge 10, at 139 miles 31 chains carried a private access to the colliery offices. Beyond this footbridge the public road to Shipley Hall crossed at 139 miles 37 chains (bridge 11). Next was the footbridge at Marlpool station (bridge 12), 139 miles 48 chains described above, and finally at Heanor station, 141 miles 0 chains (No 13) the Heanor/Derby road crossed, a short distance beyond which the branch terminated in buffer stops. Marlpool station was closed on 1st May 1928.

Fig. 263
A print from a box camera shot of the signal box and three unknown staff at Marlpool looking south. The edge of the platform awning can be seen on the left. The man in the centre is holding either the staff or a furled flag. The bridge and signal box have now gone and trees cover the area, with a path along the trackbed.

c.1900,
Courtesy Heanor Local Hist Soc

Fig. 264
A view along the Heanor branch at Level Crossing No.4, known as Meynell's Coppice crossing, looking North. The colliery on the right is Woodside, served by Shipley Collieries private lines which crossed the GN branch over bridge 9 beyond the gates. After passenger services ceased to Heanor, these gates were left open to road traffic, and operated by the train crews when necessary (see frontispiece map - Lower Erewash Valley).

1963, D H Mather

Fig. 265
This view of Shipley Collieries' locomotive *Cecil Raikes* at Coppice pit shows an unusual feature of the RCTS headboard borrowed for an enthusiasts' special along the colliery branch lines. A second colliery engine can be seen on the right. Note the stack of timber pit props beside *Cecil Raikes*.
August 1954, John R Bonser

Fig. 266
The preserved headstocks and Engine House at Woodside Colliery. The whole site of this valley and its collieries, canal and railways has been worked for opencast coal, landscaped, and is the site, after a dubious start known as Britannia Park, of the American Adventure Theme Park.

July 1981, A Henshaw

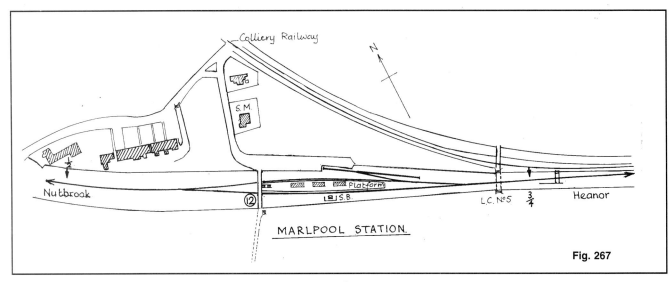

Fig. 267

110

Fig. 268
Seen from the site of signal box facing east towards Nutbrook, this shows the remains of the island platform at Marlpool and the footbridge 12 with access point to the platform but with steps removed. Thirty years later it was not possible to cross the bridge or view the site from it for trees and dense vegetation.
June 1951, F E Quenby

Fig. 269
The single line to Heanor seen from the footbridge at Marlpool station with the remains of the island platform on the left, where nature is already taking hold. The passing loop and Dock siding have been removed.
June 1951, A G Cramp

Fig. 270
This is a pen and ink drawing of Marlpool station as recalled by the artist Ian Morley of Cotmanhay near Ilkeston. He remembers the station and footbridge well from his boyhood days, and has re-created the scene with a C12 4-4-2 Tank engine leaving the island platform bunker first for Ilkeston.

c.1920, Courtesy Mark Higginson

Fig. 271
Another shot of the quite large tank engine *Cecil Raikes* which worked at Shipley Collieries for more than fifty years. Originally designed for work through the Mersey Tunnel, it bears the name of one of that company's directors. The large pipes on either side convey exhaust steam through condensers back to the water tanks, and outside frames cover the 4ft 7in diameter driving wheels, necessitating the coupling rods being outside them. The locomotive is seen at work with a background of coal wagons at Coppice Colliery.

March 1954,
John R Bonser

Fig. 272 & Fig. 273
The substantial Station Master's house at Marlpool, now fitted with modern windows and a separate sectional garage. Approval for the original plans of this building and the nearby cottages had to be given by Squire Miller Mundy of Shipley Hall. *July 1981, A Henshaw*

HEANOR for SMALLEY 141 m 8 1/2 ch

The station was opened for passengers on 1st July 1891 and for goods on 1st January 1892. There was a brick-built booking hall, booking and parcels office facing Derby Road carried on bridge 13 at the north end of the station with a covered staircase leading down to the island platform. The buildings on the bridge were similar in design to those at Eastwood, Linby and Hucknall. The platform buildings were of elaborate design in red brick with canopies supported by brackets on either side. The canopy at the south end was supported by two cast iron columns. The Station Master's house was a well-designed detached one standing on the Derby Road west of the bridge. The station was closed to ordinary passengers on 1st May 1928, but reopened with a workers' service on 18th November 1932. However this service was not advertised until 2nd October 1939, and was withdrawn on the 4th December 1939, there being a frequent bus service from the town to Derby, Ilkeston and Nottingham. It was renamed Heanor South on 1st July 1950 by British Rail.

The goods depot had a small yard with a 10-ton crane, brick built weigh office, and combined brick built shed and offices. Both Heanor and Marlpool served a wide agricultural area and there were daily forwardings of milk by passenger train to connect at Ilkeston with the milk train from Stafford to Finsbury Park.

The Ministry of Fuel and Power erected a coal screening plant for opencast coal in 1940 from which there were large forwardings by rail up to its final closure on 7th October 1963.

During the early 1970s, the Nutbrook Valley south of Woodside Colliery as far as the Ilkeston/West Hallam road was opencast mined for coal. This obliterated all the canal and railway remains. Some rectangular settlement ponds lie along the course of the Nut Brook and the northern end of the workings have been developed into the American Adventure Park with a large car park beside the preserved headstocks and engine house of Woodside Colliery. One can walk along the trackbed from the lake to the site of Marlpool station which is now minus its footbridge and well overgrown with trees and shrubs. Heanor station site is now occupied by an Industrial Estate beyond which is access to Shipley Park with its car park, and bridle roads around the site and gardens of Shipley Hall which was demolished around 1940 because of colliery subsistence.

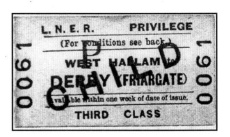

Fig. 274
This shows the arrival platform and buildings from the opencast sidings. The roof of the stairway from the road bridge can be seen above the awning. The original nameboard has gone from between the posts on the right, with the passenger station no longer in use.
June 1951, F E Quenby

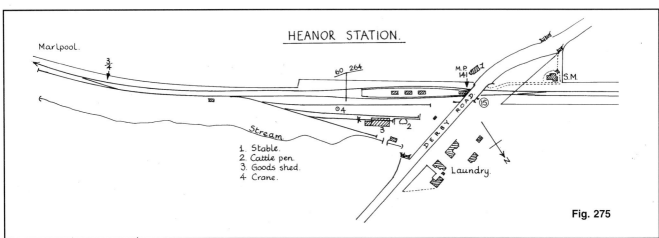

Fig. 275

Fig. 276
LNER 4032 ready to depart with its four coaches for Ilkeston. Note the slot machine immediately beyond the seat, and the two milk churns. The coaches were stabled in the bay on the down side at Ilkeston West when not in use.
December 1926, H C Casserley

Fig. 277
Originally, the two platform lines extended beyond the road, beneath bridge 15 (Fig.275) Here the train of four Howlden coaches from Ilkeston is seen at the end of the branch whilst LNER Class J3, 0-6-0 4032 is 'running round' prior to returning to the departure platform. The fencing right of the steam is the corner of the Station House garden.
December 1926, H C Casserley

Fig. 278
A good view of the goods yard and layout from above the dock (bottom left), above which can be seen the loading gauge and pillar of the hand crane. In the distance is LNER Class C12 4-4-2T 67363 with an enthusiasts' special, to the right of which are the opencast screens. Note the articulated trailer, bottom right, the power units for which were Karrier Kobs, three wheeled vehicles also called mechanical horses. Some of their trailers were converted drays.
June 1951, F E Quenby

Fig. 279
The east side elevation of the platform and buildings taken from the entrance gate and including the weighbridge platform on the left. Three wagons stand in the dock behind the cattle pen, two loaded with scrap timber.

November 1955, P Stevenson

Fig. 280
A closer view of the goods shed and office with adjacent loading gauge and iron column of the hand crane. Heanor Laundry buildings and chimney are on the right.

1963, D H Mather

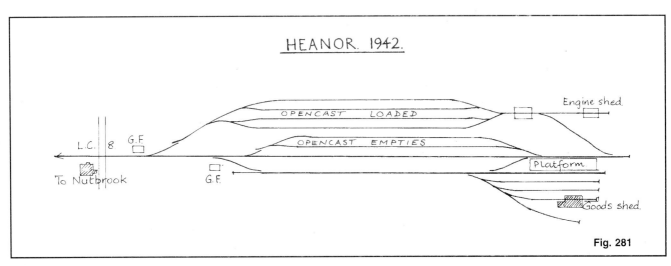

HEANOR. 1942.

Engine shed.

OPENCAST LOADED

OPENCAST EMPTIES

L.C. 8 G.F.

To Nutbrook

G.F.

Platform

Goods shed.

Fig. 281

Fig. 282
Facing south, this view shows the single line (left) and the Gatehouse at Level Crossing No.8(Heanor Coppice). The opencast sidings, laid in 1940, with two loaded wagons are on the right.

1963, D H Mather

Fig. 283
A sadly forlorn view of the station with no regular passenger service, showing BR Standard Class 2MT 2-6-2T 41320 with RCTS Special. The lines no longer extend beyond the bridge. To the left is the goods shed and dock. The NCB 0-6-0 saddle-tank engine can be seen near the screening plant (right) for loading opencast coal from the area.

September 1959, John Marshall

Fig. 284
LNER Class O4 2-8-0 63770 on the last trip up the Heanor branch. The view, facing south from near Level Crossing No.8 (Fig.282) shows the engine shunting the last opencast coal wagons to leave. It could illustrate the train departing for Ilkeston during LNER days.

1963, D H Mather

Fig. 285
The NCB standard six-coupled saddle tank locomotive at Heanor opencast site, with fire irons hanging on the cab side.

April 1956, John R Bonser

Fig. 286 & Fig. 287
The station house at Heanor Gate. The old GNR gas lamp post still stands beside an extension on the left. The building behind is a house built in the 1970s.

July 1981, A Henshaw

6. THE STANTON BRANCH

THE STANTON BRANCH

An Act of 10th August 1882 provided for a branch of 2 miles 58 1/2 chains from Stanton Junction to the Trowell Iron Company's siding and another Act of 9th May 1884 permitted a further extension of 51 chains. The branch was a single line throughout. On opening on 9th July 1883 it was worked on the system of one engine in steam accompanied by a Pilotman wearing a red band round his cap worded 'Pilotman', a red cross belt and pouch, and red armlet worded 'Pilotman' on left arm. One Pilotman worked by day and one by night between Stanton Junction and the Old and New works of the Iron Company. Points at Derby Road and Ilkeston Colliery sidings were locked by special keys carried by the Pilotmen. At 6.0 am on Monday 5th August 1901, Pilotman working was replaced by a square-shaped staff lettered "Stanton Branch" on both sides and kept at Stanton Junction signal box. Working to Stanton Ironworks was one brake van in front and two in the rear, the order being reversed on return. The points on the branch were now secured by locks released by the train staff, and no engine or train was to pass Derby Road without stopping for the guard to pin down necessary brakes before descending the 1 in 70 incline into the Ironworks.

Fig. 288
Approximately half a mile from Stanton Junction. the Stanton branch passes beneath the Derby Road (A609) from Ilkeston and here was built a small goods and coal depot, called Derby Rd. The entrance, from east of bridge 4, was through a gate, adjacent to which was the usual type of weighbridge and office, seen here.
August 1981, A Henshaw

DERBY ROAD GOODS DEPOT 138 m 2 1/4 ch

This small yard was opened on 9th July 1883, south of the Ilkeston-Derby road. It had a loading deck at the north end, and a slate roofed timber goods shed with combined office at the other end. A cart weighbridge with red brick office of standard design was built just inside the entrance gate off Derby Road. The site continued in use by coal merchants until the 1980s but was derelict by 1992.

A third system of operating the branch came into operation on 2nd April 1923 consisting of Electric Token Block Instruments between Stanton Junction and the Fork Junction cabin in the Ironworks.

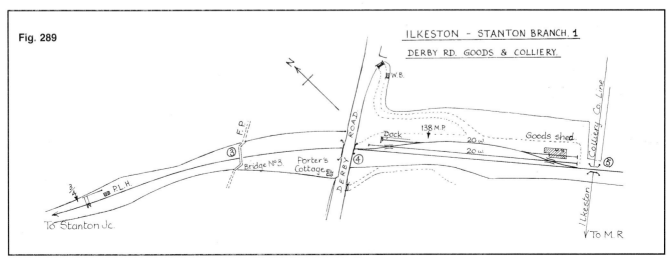

Fig. 289

ILKESTON - STANTON BRANCH. 1
DERBY RD. GOODS & COLLIERY.

Fig. 290
This early photograph of bridge 4, looking north towards Stanton Junction, shows the Porter's Cottage on the left, and the footbridge 3 through the span. To the right of the double slip points can be seen the brickwork of the dock. Point rodding from the ground frame near the bridge is on the left.
c.1910,
Courtesy British Rail

Fig. 291
The view of Derby Road, Ilkeston, from bridge 4 on the Stanton branch, with a diesel-hauled train of iron ore ready to depart down the 1 in 70 gradient to Quarry Hill Road. The guard is climbing aboard, having pinned down the necessary brakes. The extra siding serving the goods shed and dock has long since been lifted, but there is activity amongst the coal merchants on the left.
c. 1955, P Stevenson

Fig. 292
A little way south of Derby Road Goods the Stanton branch crossed the Midland Railway's branch to Oakwell and Ilkeston Colliery by bridge 5. Needless to say, the GNR built connections to both the colliery and the brick and clay pipe works. This view looking north shows the connections to Oakwell pipe siding left, and the colliery right, from beside bridge 6 over an occupation road to Oakwell Farm and the 138 1/4 mile post. Oakwell brickworks were on the left.
November 1955, P Stevenson

Fig. 293
This shows the southern end of Derby Road Goods at Ilkeston with the wooden goods shed and sidings still in use. Derby Road crosses the branch by bridge 4, the town being to the right and West Hallam to the left.
November 1955, P Stevenson

Fig. 294
A view along the B6001 road at Little Hallam Hill facing east where it is crossed by the Stanton branch on bridge 8. Subsequent timber strengthening has been added.
January 1968, A Henshaw

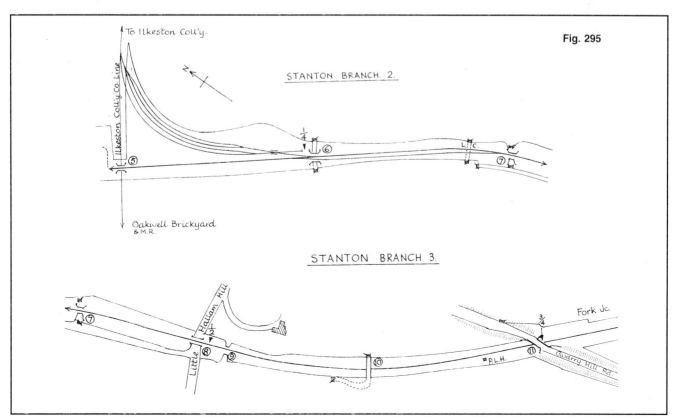

Fig. 295

To Ilkeston Coll'y.

STANTON BRANCH. 2.

N

Ilkeston Coll'y Co. Line

⑤

Oakwell Brickyard & M.R.

L.C.

⑥

⑦

STANTON BRANCH 3.

Little Hallam Hill

⑦

⑧

⑨

⑩

⑪

P.L.H.

Fork Jc.

Quarry Hill Rd.

Fig. 296
Approaching Quarry Hill Ground Frame, this view shows the home signals. Through bridge 11 left of the track the low dark building houses the ground frame, which was opened by BR in 1959 and named Quarry Hill Road. The chimney and Coking Plant appear faintly above the signal box/ground frame.
January 1968, A Henshaw

Fig. 297
Quarry Hill Ground Frame cabin seen from the sidings which served the ore preparation plant. The store of ironstone is partly seen on the left. After crushing, some of this ore was sent to Staveley Works *via* Bulwell Common and Chesterfield GC.

January 1968, A Henshaw

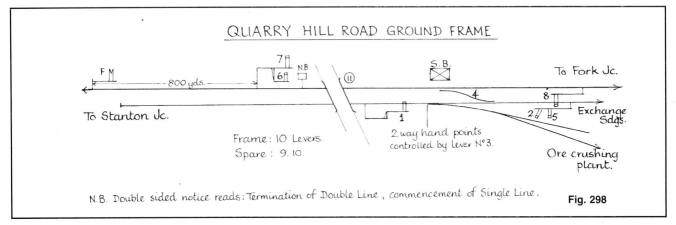

QUARRY HILL ROAD GROUND FRAME

Frame: 10 Levers.
Spare: 9. 10.

2 way hand points controlled by lever Nº 3.

To Stanton Jc.

To Fork Jc.

Exchange Sdgs.

Ore crushing plant.

N.B. Double sided notice reads: Termination of Double Line, commencement of Single Line.

Fig. 298

QUARRY HILL ROAD GROUND FRAME 138 m 62 1/2 ch

Quarry Hill Road Ground Frame was opened in 1959. The electric key token instrument was transferred from Fork Junction cabin to this box and trains were then worked between these two points by fixed signals, but siding accommodation continued to be built to serve the ore preparation plant until 1960. It was closed officially on 6th May 1968, but after this it was re-connected and used for recovery of track from GNR and GC lines of the Leen Valley and the GNR Derbyshire Extension including the Stanton Branch itself, by T W Ward & Co. The whole site to Fork Junction has been cleared and is occupied by the Quarry Hill Industrial Park of single storey buildings.

Fig. 299
A view from bridge 11, facing SE, showing LNER Class O4/8 2-8-0 63657 idling past before arriving at the works with a train of ore. The embankment beyond the tender has been cut away in preparation for the building of Quarry Hill Road Ground Frame cabin, two pieces of equipment for which are standing beside the track. The coking plant ovens are on the right above the fulls coal sidings. The 3 blast furnaces of the New Works can be seen between the tree and the column of steam from the safety valve.
1958, J F Henton

Fig. 300
Another view of the Ground Frame cabin from the branch home signal, which shows a rebuilt LNER Class O4 2-8-0 arriving from Stanton Junction with a mineral train. The signalman stands outside the cabin prepared to take the electric token from the fireman. The sidings left lead to the ore preparation plant.
August 1962, A Henshaw

FORK JUNCTION 139 m 16 ch

From here, the branch continued and swung left to Hallam Fields siding to serve Trowell Forge and Ironworks, and the New Works furnaces. In 1938 the coking plant was built with 41 ovens and sidings for holding coal and empties. This was extended to a further 44 ovens in 1951, surplus gas being fed into the grid of the East Midlands Gas Board.

The Coking Plant at Hallam Fields was separated from both Old and New Works furnaces by the old GNR lines New Works branch. Coke for the Old Works was worked *via* Fork Junction, and the GNR until the Stanton Company laid a connecting line between the New Works sidings of the GNR and Midland lines in 1947.

Another branch swung to the right and climbed steeply over the Midland Railway's branch to Mapperley Colliery, and the Nutbrook Canal to serve the Old Works, Pipe sidings and Dale sidings. This branch, authorised on 19th May 1884 was completed in 1885. The working at Fork Junction was controlled by Inspectors, who kept two tablets; one for each branch. The first one was square-shaped, lettered "New Yard New Works to Stanton Works Junction" and the second one was round-shaped, lettered "Old Yard Old Works to Stanton Works Junction". Originally the working from Stanton Junction was to Fork Junction but the electric token block section was shortened with the opening of Quarry Road Ground Frame, and instruments transferred from Fork Junction cabin to Quarry Hill Road.

A new Iron Refining Plant was opened in 1964 on the north side of Lowe's Lane and west of the GNR bridge 4 beneath the road. The Stanton Company then purchased the Old Works branch from Fork Junction to the Dale spun pipe sidings from British Rail. On Whit Tuesday 16th May 1964 the branch was severed at bridge 1 over the Midland Railway. A new curve connected the Refining Plant to the branch at bridge 4 for the conveyance of molten metal to the spun pipe plant south of Lowe's Lane. This was then the only remaining part of the old GNR in the Works .

After severance at bridge 1, British Rail laid a link siding from the GN branch at Fork Junction to the Midland Railway's Mapperley branch at New Works sidings signal box. This line opened on 27th May.

Iron ore from Leicestershire and Northamptonshire could not compete with imported ores from Sweden and Spain for quality, and this traffic previously handled by the GNR dwindled in the 1960s. The new Refining Plant used scrap metal for its production, and the furnaces closed down. Final remodelling involved the closure of Quarry Hill Ground Frame on 19th May 1968 for an extension of the Bottom Empty sidings to join the Through Siding, as the branch was then named.

Now, the branch has been removed, the ore preparation plant dismantled, and a new Industrial Park with single-storey units occupies the area east of Quarry Hill Road. Along the branch serving the New Works, bridge 13 from Compton Street has been removed, leaving reduced abutments; footbridge 14 has also been demolished, and bridge 15 at Hallam Fields has been packed with earth. The schools are replaced by new single-storey factories and offices which occupy the site of the old GNR sidings and branch both sides of the bridge.

After this all traffic was carried by road to the old works spun iron plant. Early in 1998 Stanton plc (producing some 100,000 tons of ductile iron pipes a year) submitted a scheme to reinstate the former MR rail connection from beside Lowes Lane to Stanton Gate. This has been laid as a single line siding crossing Littlemill Lane where the hut formerly controlling the traffic had been demolished (Fig.311 p128). A Class 56 diesel locomotive was named STANTON at Toton by EWS (English, Welsh and Scottish Railways) chief executive Ed Burkhardt and Stanton chairman Geoff Nicholls in September 1998.

A trial run from Toton Sidings to Plymouth with a train 1/4 mile long which conveyed 3/4 mile of pipes for a water pipeline project was made on 26 September 1996.

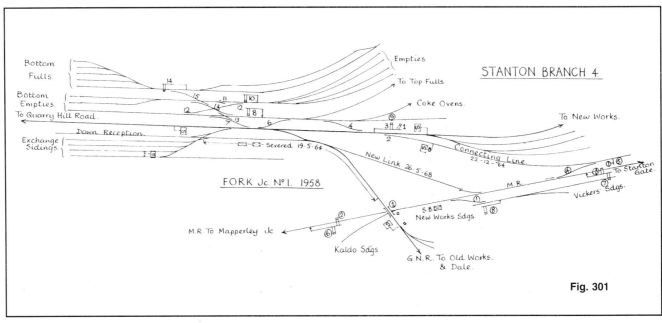

Fig. 301

124

Fig. 302
This view facing east towards Fork Junction along the GN branch to New Works shows the illuminated STOP board for trains leaving New Works sidings (Fig.301 P124). In the distance, centre, are the signals Nos.1 and 3. The ore preparation plant is on the left, and beside the pipe there, is the new connecting line to the MR sidings at New Works. No.3 signal being 'off' indicates that the road is set for the new line from Fork Junction.

January 1968, A Henshaw

Fig. 303
Looking east along the MR branch to Mapperley Junction, through bridge 1 over which the GNR reached the Old Works and Spun Pipe plant from Fork Junction. On the right are the new Ore Preparation plant and the overhead conveyor which serves it. The Ground Frame on the left controlled entrance to the Kaldo Plant sidings beyond the bridge. Note the steep gradient each side.

January 1968, A Henshaw

Fig. 304
Fork Junction facing Quarry Hill Road. The curve bottom centre leads to the Top Full Sidings of the Coking Plant. The straight line is the New Works branch and on the adjacent embankment beside the signal post is the new Link Line to the MR New Works Sidings signal box. The Ore Preparation Plant forms the background, its conveyor belt bridging the tracks.

January 1968, A Henshaw

Fig. 305
LNER class O4 63644, and BR class 9F 92044 standing on the Down reception road at Fork Junction, obscuring the Ground frame Signal Box. Behind 63644 is the ore preparation plant.
October 1963, P Stevenson

Fig. 306
Seen from the Pipe Sidings entrance in the Old Works is bridge 3 across the Nutbrook Canal (Fig.309) which carried the GN branch from Fork Junction to the Old Works and Dale Sidings where the Spun Pipe works were built. This was a tricky section to work because of curves and severe gradients needed to cross over the Midland Rly branch. In 1964 the Stanton Company purchased this branch from BR and severed the connection from Fork Junction prior to where it crossed the Midland branch. The length from the Melting Plant and Spun Pipe works beneath Lowes Lane was used to transfer hot metal to the Old Works after more internal modifications to the track layout. Beyond the bridge on the right can be seen the ore crushing and preparation plant.
January 1968, A Henshaw

Fig. 307
The same bridge as above viewed from the opposite bank of the canal, showing the Kaldo Converter plant on the left. The ends of the girders have been strengthened with concrete above the abutments, for this bridge suffered slight damage from bombs dropped by German Zeppelin raids in 1916. Note the square door in the middle of the girder for fire hose access to the canal below. The branch curves round to Lowes Lane and the Spun Pipe plant at Dale from the left hand side of this photograph.
July 1969, A Henshaw

Fig. 308
The Kaldo smelting plant facing west, showing the rail connections. The curve to the left leads to the spun pipe works and passes beneath Lowes Lane bridge. The lines to the right connected with the engine shed and repair shops, and extended to the Midland Erewash Valley lines at Stanton Gate.

January 1992, A Henshaw

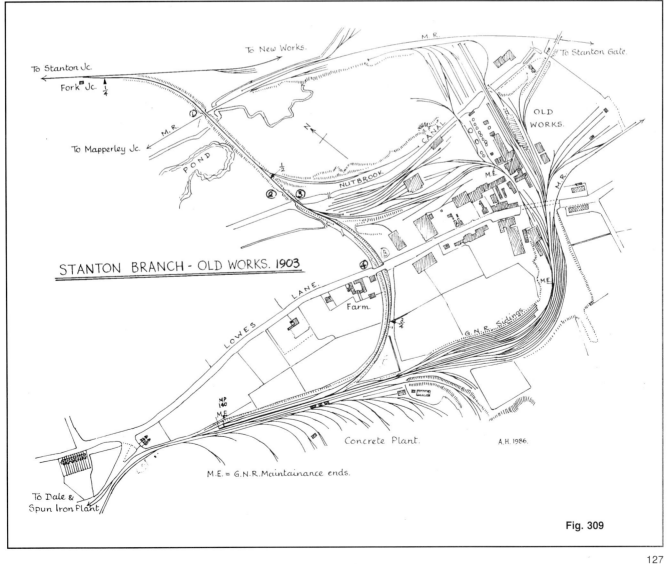

STANTON BRANCH - OLD WORKS. 1903

M.E. = G.N.R. Maintainance ends.

Fig. 309

Fig. 310
A relaxed looking guard on the return from the Spun Pipe works about to pass beneath Lows Lane bridge 4. The old farm buildings can been seen on the left.

October 1963, P. Stevenson

Fig. 311
Lowes Lane bottom foreground at the junction with Littlewell Lane right, across which is the Stanton Company's own line to Dale guarded by the tall building left of the concrete lamppost but not by gates! Well built and maintained company cottages stand on the left in front of the line.

January 1992, A Henshaw

Fig. 312
Looking across Lowes Lane the stack yard for concrete spun pipes fronting the road is seen here, with the plant building behind.

January 1992, A. Henshaw

Fig. 313
The continuation of the branch beneath Lowes Lane towards Dale, passing first stacks of iron pipes, and second the spun concrete pipes. To the right of the pipes can be seen the box which controlled the level crossing at Littlewell Lane, which leads to Stanton-by-Dale village. The stacks of concrete pipes stretch beyond Littlewell Lane.

January 1992, A Henshaw

Fig. 314
View facing NE from South of bridge 13 showing New Works furnaces beneath the overhead furnace gas pipeline. The lines in the foreground are from the MR branch to the New Works; the connection from the GN branch and sidings leads in from the left immediately behind the central stanchion and the wagons. The damaged signal probably controlled entrance to the GN at one time. The line sloping upwards in the distance, immediately right of the central stanchion is the charging line to the furnaces from which coke, ore and limestone were fed.

January 1968, A Henshaw

Fig. 315
View from the footbridge between School Lane and Crompton Street (built after 1904) facing SW which shows wagons of coke in the GN sidings, now spanned by a covered conveyor belt for feeding ore from the preparation plant near Quarry Road to the furnaces. Sloping up to the left above the two hopper wagons is the charging line mentioned in Fig.314. The two lines which curve to the right are the branch from Fork Junction. to beyond bridge 15 at Hallam Fields Road.

January 1968, A Henshaw

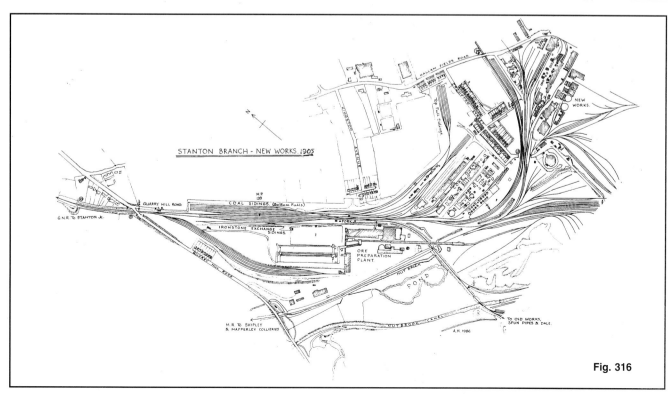

STANTON BRANCH - NEW WORKS. 1905

Fig. 316

Fig. 317
Moving in front of a stack of sleeved pipes at South View, near the end of Crompton Street, an unidentified industrial locomotive is seen. Behind the sheds and workshop are the New works blast furnaces.
March 1956, John R Bonser

Fig. 318
The new link between Fork Junction Old Works branch and the Midland Railway branch from Stanton Gate to Shipley and Mapperley Collieries with two Class 20 diesels arriving. It was opened in May 1968 to enable traffic to reach Quarry Hill Road sidings from Stanton Gate MR, after closure of the GNR branch. This view shows the bridge across the Nutbrook in the foreground; New Works Plant on the left and the train of coal is passing New Works sidings MR Signal Box, behind which is the overhead conveyor from the ore preparation plant to the furnaces. The large gas holder is framed in the gantry.
1968, P Stevenson

Fig. 319
The end of the branch to New Works at Hallam Fields, seen from bridge 15, facing north. When planned, it was intended to serve Trowell Forge, whose building can be seen in the distance, right of the tracks. Before the line was completed however, the owners of the forge became bankrupt, and the line was terminated just beyond the bridge. The centre buildings in the distance are houses at the Forge, and on the left is the Eagle Mill at Trowell.
January 1968, A Henshaw

Fig. 320
Seen beside the water softeners at the Old Works furnaces are two of the many industrial locomotives owned by the Stanton Ironworks Company. First is 22, an 0-6-0 side tank made by Dick Kerr of Kilmarnock in 1915, and purchased from the ROD at Chilwell. It went for scrap at Oakwell in 1958. Behind it is the front of 38, another six-coupled tank engine, made by Andrew Barclay in 1949 and acquired new from the makers whose number was 2273. This engine was scrapped in the 1960s.

August 1955,
John R Bonser

Fig. 321
Bridge 11 on the branch from Stanton Junction at Quarry Hill Road is now filled in with earth packing and fenced off along the road sides. This is the view facing east from the bridge, showing the recent light industrial buildings in Quarry Hill Industrial Park, which covers the site of the sidings to the ore preparation plant. On the extreme right is the Kaldo smelting plant.
January 1992, A Henshaw

Fig. 322
This aerial view looking north is of the New Works furnaces and the Nutbrook Plant, which made small pipes and specials, junctions, etc. Prominent on the left is the large gas holder, behind which is the overhead conveyor from the preparation plant.

Top left is a cloud of steam from the coke ovens, and Hallam Fields Road. Note the new factories opposite the older terraced houses behind which are a few wagons in the Top Full Sidings holding a few wagons. Further right is the sweep of the Erewash Canal, the Midland Railway's Erewash Valley lines and the branch from Trowell Junction through Wollaton to Radford Junction. The GNR branch from Fork Junction enters behind the gasholder, and beneath the overhead pipeline, curving left beneath the conveyor and passing behind the tall chimney, where more wagons can be seen. Bridge 15 at Hallam Fields can be seen near the junction with Crompton Street and the school buildings are at that corner.

The lower part of the picture shows the slag crushing and preparation plant, which produced road-building material. This is not included in the plan of the New Works (Fig. 316 P.129).

Ctsy D Corns/Stanton Co

Fig. 323
Facing east, this picture of the Old Works furnaces shows Lowes Lane to their left, running from top to bottom, where the right hand turn to Crompton Street joins. The ore preparation plant occupies the top right corner, with Fork Junction beneath its smoke. From here the curve of the Old Works branch passes beneath the large conveyor, with bridge 1 spanning the Midland Railway trackbed immediately to its left. The GNR track has been removed also, but the bridge over the Nutbrook Canal still stands. Above, and left of the canal is the Kaldo or Refining plant opened in 1964, from which a rail link curves left to pass beneath Lowes Lane by the old GNR track to the spun iron plant.

Ctsy D Corns/Stanton Co

133

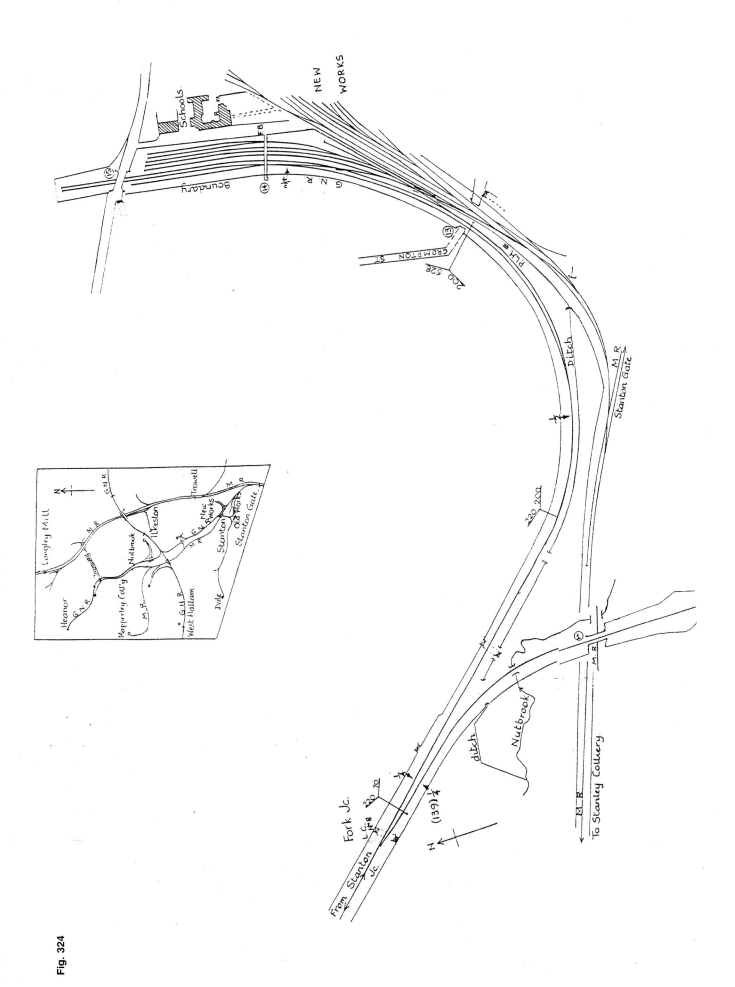

Fig. 324

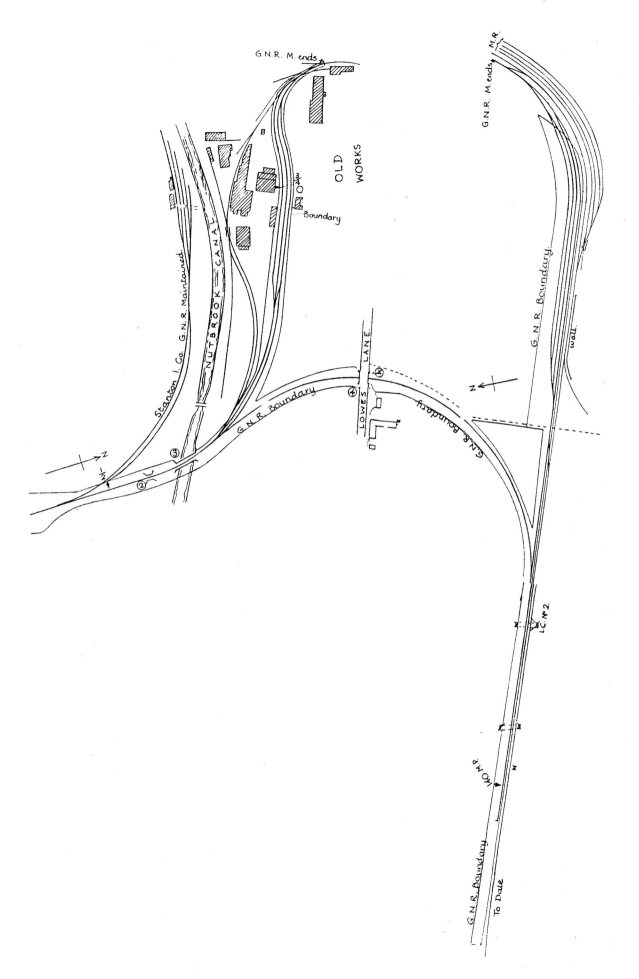

Fig. 324

Fig. 325
This is a view of the Stanhope, or 18ft plant of the concrete works which was built opposite the GNR sidings, south of the Old Works along Lowes Lane. The farm and Lowes Lane with bridge 4 and the curve of the old GNR Old Works branch beneath it are in the top right hand corner; the top left hand corner being approximately where the GNR maintenance ended. Stanton's own lines continued beyond this to the Spun Iron plant and its earlier quarries and works at Dale. The large stock yard for pipes is clearly seen at the top left.
Ctsy D Corns/ Stanton Co

(9402)

Immediate

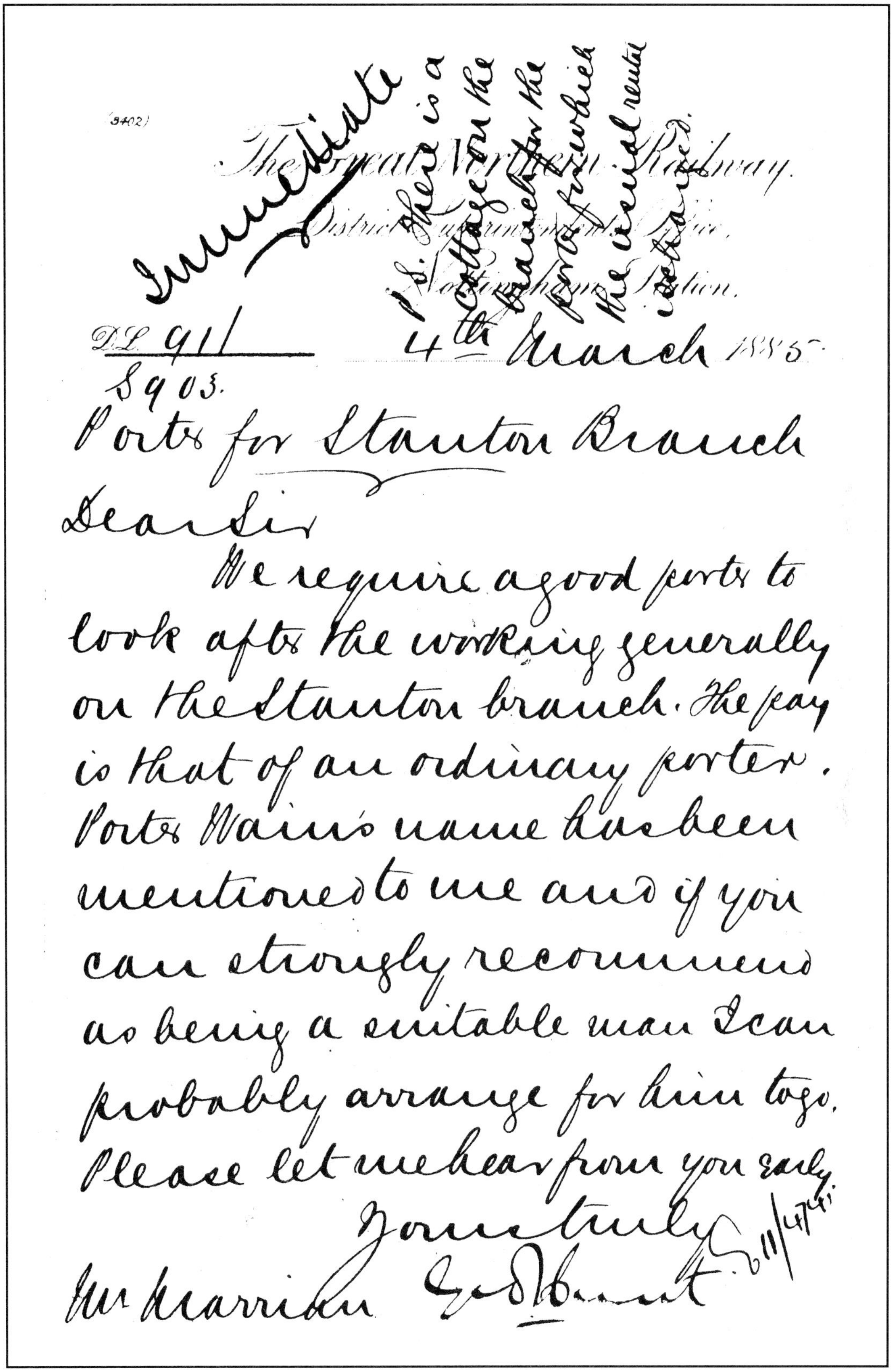

The Great Northern Railway.
District Superintendent's Office,
Nottingham Station.

There is a
Cottage on the
branch for
Porter for which
the usual rents

DL 911
8903.

4th March 1885

Porter for Stanton Branch

Dear Sir

We require a good porter to
look after the working generally
on the Stanton branch. The pay
is that of an ordinary porter.
Porter Wain's name has been
mentioned to me and if you
can strongly recommend
as being a suitable man I can
probably arrange for him to go.
Please let me hear from you early.

Yours truly

11/4/91

Mr Harrison

Appendix 1
Extract from a résumé of the railway career of the late William Charles Cresswell at Pye Hill and Somercotes from 1938 to 1941.

We moved from Halstead in January 1938 to the Station House at Pye Hill. What a change in surroundings, looking out on to colliery tips, smoking chimneys and just across one field a tar distillery and acid works and I discovered one if not the worst valley for fog in the country, the Erewash Valley. The family now consisted of four, two daughters aged 8 and 2 years old besides ourselves. We soon adapted ourselves to what seemed an almost foreign country at first.

My duties at the station which was situated on the side of a very steep hill, I found quite interesting and as the line was double was something I had not previously had experience of, from a working point of view. The train service consisted of 18 trains daily with two extra on Wednesdays and four extra on Saturdays between the hours of 6am to 10.30pm and used by a large number of passengers especially early morning and evening, consisting mostly of workgirls to and from Nottingham and suburbs. Merchandise traffic catered for was sectional concrete articles, composition flooring and wall tiles, and hosiery and woollen underwear, the latter including some well known brands.

The station was also connected by siding to two collieries, Pye Hill and New Selston where about 100 wagons of coal a day were loaded. The Midland Main line station at Pye Bridge was alongside about 50 yards away.

Our nearest Congregational Church was at Riddings just over the border in Derbyshire, to which our membership was transferred from Halstead. It was while living here that I was approached to give talks to the Men's Fellowship on railway subjects.

The whole district in many respects was most interesting to me from a work as well as leisure angle. It was quite near Chesterfield and the Derbyshire Dales, Mansfield and the Dukeries and the city of Nottingham but our stay there, only three and a half years, was greatly marred by the restrictions of the Second World War. It was an entirely new experience for me to be living and working in a colliery district and as previously mentioned we felt very strange but we soon made friendships which still exist.

I was enabled to visit the underground workings of Langton Colliery, one of the Pinxton Group, on a Sunday, a really wonderful experience. During the winter of 1940, a heavy snowstorm came on during a Saturday night and early Sunday morning we woke up to find everywhere snowbound and on opening the door discovered snow more than half way up the door and I had to dig my way out, with a small coal shovel to get a spade. For the whole of the day we were isolated and I spent all day until after dark clearing tracks to enable passengers to get to the station early on Monday. Such conditions existed for several weeks and sickness among staff was rife especially among the signalling staff and so many were absent that for a fortnight I had to work the signal box myself in addition to my own duties. Apart from this and a few derailments in the sidings everything went off fairly smoothly. By June 1941 I had been promoted to Langrick Station near Boston in Lincolnshire and moved to take up this appointment in September 1941.

Appendix 2
Collieries Served by GNR/LNER Nottingham Area

OWNER	COLLIERY	STATION	SUNK / OPEN	CLOSED / MERGED (M)
Awsworth C Co	Awsworth	Awsworth	1875/7	1898
TN	Babbington	Basford & Bulwell	1852	Feb 1986
BW	Brinsley	Eastwood & Langley Mill	1872	(M) Moorgreen 1918 1934
TN	Broxtowe	Basford & Bulwell	1863	1949
PX	Brookhill	Kirkby Bentinck	1909	1968
JO	Clifton/Stoneyford	Eastwood & Langley Mill	Before 1853	1887
Shipley	Coppice	Ilkeston	1875	1966
Digby	Digby	Newthorpe	1866	1937
BW	Eastwood (Manson)	Newthorpe	1834	1884
TN	Hempshill (Babbington)	Basford & Bulwell	1837/8	(M) Babbington before 1853
BW	High Park	Eastwood & Langley Mill	1861	1944
Ilkeston C Co	Ilkeston	Ilkeston	1874	1912
TN	Kimberley	Basford & Bulwell	1855/60	1907
PX	Langton	Kirkby Bentinck	1880	(M) Bentinck 1967
W Hall	Lodge	Newthorpe	1878	1960
Manners C Co	Manners	Ilkeston	1877	1949
BW	Moorgreen	Eastwood & Langley Mill	1868	1985
TN	Newcastle	Basford & Bulwell	1853	1929
Digby	New London	Newthorpe	1878	(M) Digby 1927
J Shorthose	Peacock	Ilkeston	1875	1896
PX	Pinxton 2 & 6	Pinxton	1836	(M) Brookhill 1950
Pinxton Tar Distillers	Pinxton Coke Ovens	Pinxton	c.1905	1956
JO	Pollington	Codnor Park	1876	1920
JO	Pye Hill	Codnor Park	1875	1985
JO	Riddings	Codnor Park	Before 1853	1904
Shipley	Shipley	Ilkeston	1871	1935
Digby	Speedwell	Newthorpe	1870	(M) Digby 1887
BW	Underwood (Pye Hill 2)	Eastwood & Langley Mill	1852	1983
BW	Watnall (New)	Kimberley	1875	1952
Shipley	Woodside 1	Ilkeston	1848	1928
Shipley	Woodside 2 & 3	Ilkeston	1899	1961
Shipley	Nutbrook	Ilkeston	Before 1880	1895

TN	=	Thomas North
BW	=	Barber Walker
PX	=	Pinxton Collieries
JO	=	James Oakes

Appendix 3A
Giltbrook Viaduct (Kimberley Viaduct)

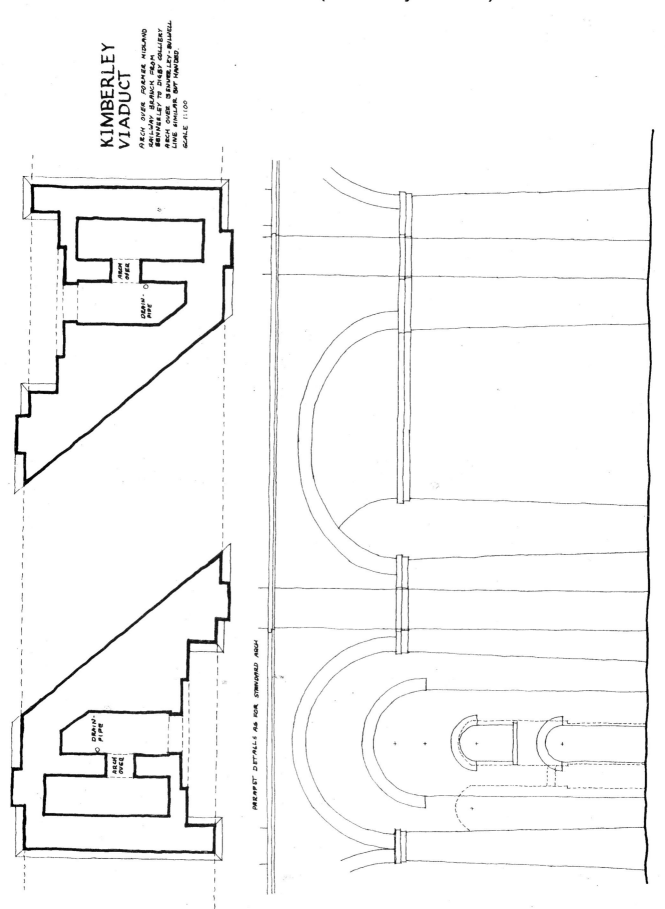

KIMBERLEY VIADUCT

ARCH OVER FORMER MIDLAND RAILWAY BRANCH FROM BENNERLEY TO DIGBY COLLIERY
ARCH OVER BENNERLEY-BULWELL LINE SIMILAR BUT HANDED.
SCALE 1:100

ARCH OVER

DRAIN-PIPE

DRAIN-PIPE

ARCH OVER

PARAPET DETAILS AS FOR STANDARD ARCH

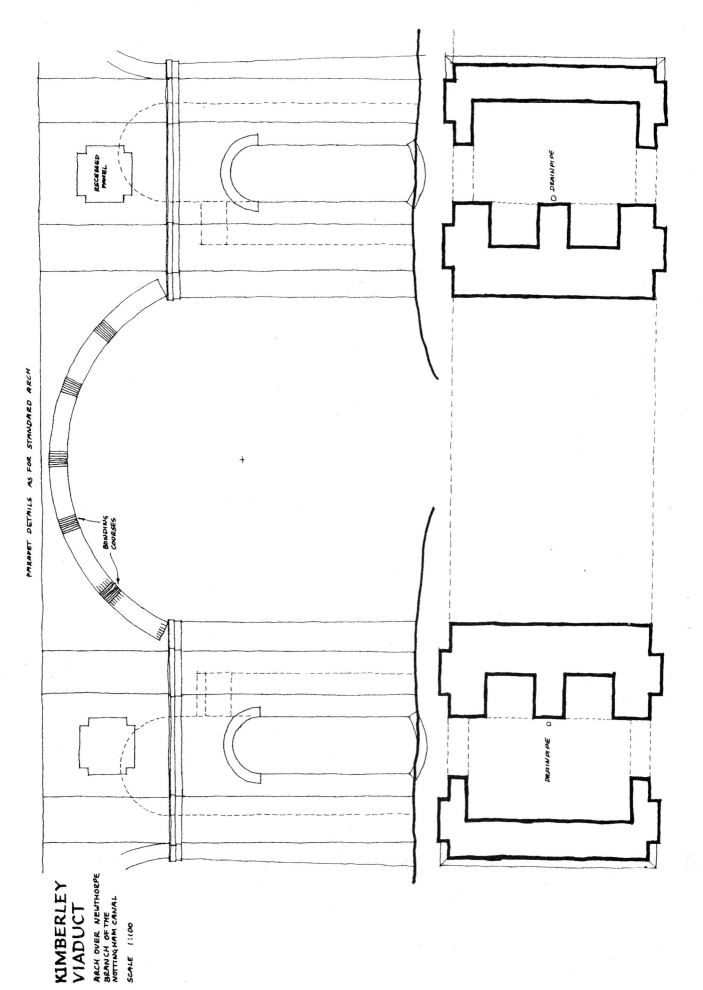

KIMBERLEY
VIADUCT

ARCH OVER NEWTHORPE
BRANCH OF THE
NOTTINGHAM CANAL

SCALE 1:100

PARAPET DETAILS AS FOR STANDARD ARCH

RECESSED
PANEL

BONDING
COURSES

DRAIN PIPE

DRAIN PIPE

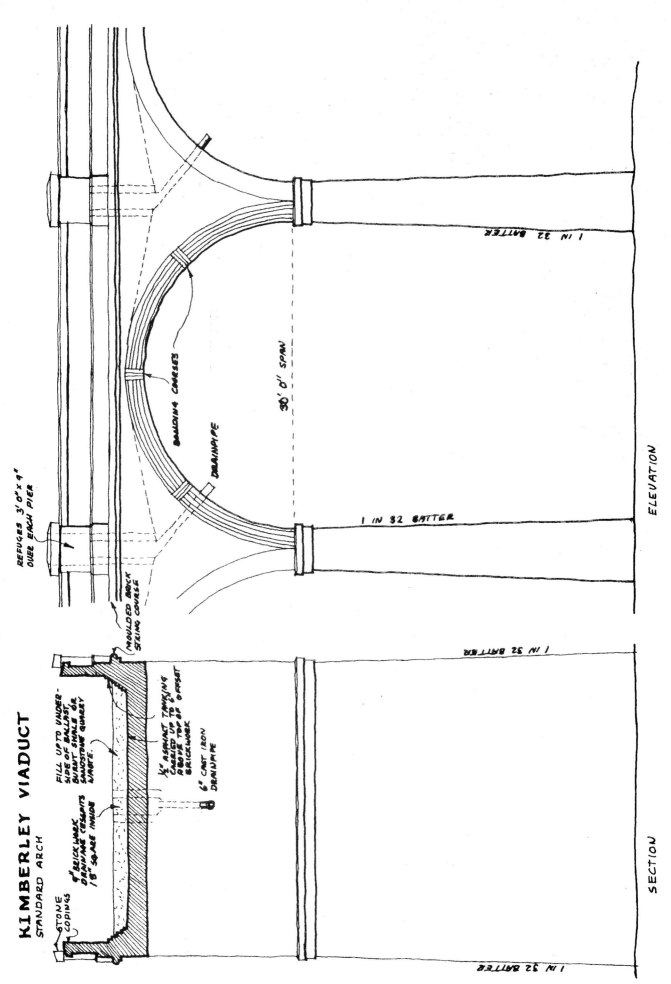

KIMBERLEY VIADUCT
STANDARD ARCH

STONE COPINGS

9" BRICKWORK DRAINING CESSPITS 18" SQUARE INSIDE

FILL UP TO UNDER-SIDE OF BALLAST BURNT SHALE OR SANDSTONE QUARRY WASTE.

½" ASPHALT TANKING CARRIED UP TO 6" ABOVE TOP OF OFFSET BRICKWORK

6" CAST IRON DRAINPIPE

REFUGES 3'0" x 4' OVER EACH PIER

MOULDED BRICK STRING COURSE

BANDING COURSES

DRAINPIPE

30' 0" SPAN

1 IN 32 BATTER

1 IN 32 BATTER

ELEVATION

1 IN 32 BATTER

1 IN 32 BATTER

SECTION

142

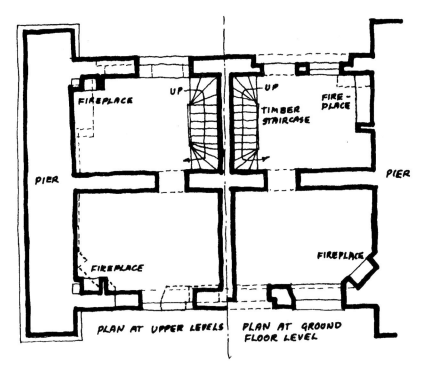

KIMBERLEY VIADUCT

BUILT-UP ARCHES, FORMERLY USED AS COTTAGES

FIREPLACES ON EACH FLOOR DISCHARGED INTO A COMMON FLUE CARRIED UP WITHIN THE THICKNESS OF THE PARAPET

FLOORS WERE OF TIMBER BOARDING AND JOISTS. LATH AND PLASTER CEILINGS

FIREPLACE

FIREPLACE

UP

UP

TIMBER STAIRCASE

FIRE-PLACE

PIER

PIER

FIREPLACE

FIREPLACE

PLAN AT UPPER LEVELS

PLAN AT GROUND FLOOR LEVEL

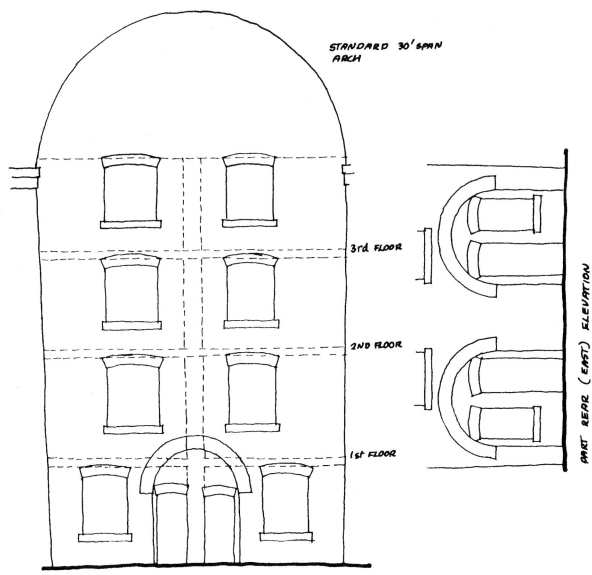

STANDARD 30' SPAN ARCH

3rd FLOOR

2ND FLOOR

1st FLOOR

FRONT (WEST) ELEVATION

PART REAR (EAST) ELEVATION

Appendix 3B
A REPORT ON THE GENERAL CONDITION OF THE KIMBERLEY (GILTBROOK) VIADUCT

The main points of the general condition of this viaduct have already been covered in an earlier report by Mr N. Summers. The viaduct, on the former Great Northern Railway Kimberley-Pinxton branch is about 540 yards long, forming a shallow S-curve in plan, and consists of 47 arches which vary in span from 25 to 44 feet (7.625 m - 13.42 m.), but most of them are of 30 feet (9.15 m.) span, and are about 45 feet (13.72 m.) high. The track has been lifted and the ballast removed, leaving just the filling above the arches, which consists of burnt colliery shale at the north end and sandstone quarry waste at the south end. The parapets have been all but destroyed in places, apparently by slewing rails during track removal operations.

The track drainage system is in need of repair. In the centre of the track above each pier there is a brick catchpit 18" square internally and constructed of 9" brickwork. These catchpits collect the drainage water from the track and discharge it under each arch by a 6" cast iron pipe. They have been packed solid with debris, though the water apparently still percolates through. The whole of the top of the arches has been waterproofed with a $\frac{1}{2}$" layer of bitumen. This appears to be functioning properly where it is covered by the filling, but is coming away from the brickwork at the base of the parapets where it is now exposed.

There are two skew arches of 25 feet span on the square, both over former railways, and a large arch of 44 feet span over the course of the Newthorpe branch of the Nottingham Canal. All these arches are flanked by massive piers which are hollow. Those belonging to the skew arches are particularly complicated in design, and have two chambers side by side, but only one is open to the outside. In one of these chambers there is a drainpipe from the track, and water dripping from this has soaked the brickwork, which has then been attacked by frost, causing severe cracking and spalling. Such brickwork would have to be cut out and rebuilt, and the drainpipe extended down to ground level and the water properly drained away. The same sort of thing has happened in the hollow abutments on either side of the canal arch and would be dealt with similarly.

Besides these arches there are two of the 'standard' arches which have been built up at sometime, probably at the time the viaduct was built. They are divided into four rooms on each of four floors. The rooms have plastered walls and ceilings, and the upper floors had timber floors. Fireplaces in each room discharged into a common flue at each corner of the area covered by the arch. The flues were carried up through the thickness of the arch and into hollow piers on the parapets. The rooms are said to have been used as cottages and school rooms. Rather steep and narrow timber staircases ran from floor to floor. The rooms are now completely derelict. Nearly all the woodwork has gone, and a little remains of the upper floors. Much of the plaster has fallen away, and the chimneys are choked with debris. There is evidence of water damage in one of the arches.

These built-up arches are probably essential to the structure of the viaduct. The piers generally are too slender to act as abutments, and in the event of failure of one of the arches, progressive collapse of the rest would follow unless there were piers at intervals, strong enough to act as abutments. The skew arch abutments serve well in this respect, but in the built-up arches the walls act as diaphragms which prevent the arch from any tendency to deform or the piers to overturn, so the arches are in effect abutments.

The viaduct is built of rough handmade common bricks, which except for the frost damage, are generally in good condition. The mortar has not fared so well and much pointing needs to be done, especially at high level. The coping stones which have fallen should be collected and stored for re-use. Some bricks could be re-used, but new bricks should be the pressed colliery shale common bricks made locally by the N.C.B. as these match the existing ones closest in colour and texture. In the built-up arches the remaining timber floors should be removed and the chimneys sealed off and the whole generally tidied up. The ground floor should be paved with concrete, as should be the floors of the chambers in the skew arch piers. These are of bare earth strewn with rubbish at the moment. At track level, all the drainage catchpits need to be cleaned out and provided with covers to suit whatever paving is eventually used. The width between the parapets is 25'8" (7.825 m.) is really too narrow for a road, of any size. If the viaduct is laid out as a promenade, a fine few can be enjoyed by those who move along it at a leisurely pace. A walk should also be made at ground level so that the fine engineering can be appreciated from below.

Some long stretches of parapet will need to be completely rebuilt. There are the stumps of two signal posts bolted to the parapet near the south end, which need to be removed.

Personally, I think this viaduct is a fine piece of engineering, and I should like to see it preserved. When inspecting the details of construction, I tried to see what the engineer's design problems were and how he solved them. The result, translated into bricks and mortar, is what we see today. The design and construction of such large brick structures is now a lost art, so let us keep this example, the best in this area, of that art.

M.D.P. Hammond
3rd May 1970

GREAT NORTHERN RAILWAY.

NOTICE.

Circular No. 2008a.

DERBYSHIRE EXTENSION.

SPECIAL NOTICE.

No Engine or Train, either Up or Down, must run at a higher rate of speed than 20 Miles per hour between the Ilkeston East Signal Box, and the Awsworth Sidings Signal Box.

Double Line is now open throughout between Tutbury, Derby and Awsworth Junction.

Circular No. 1960A is cancelled.

FRANCIS P. COCKSHOTT,
Superintendent of the Line.

SUPERINTENDENT'S OFFICE,
KING'S CROSS,
March 25th, 1878.

Appendix 4A
Ilkeston (Bennerley) Viaduct

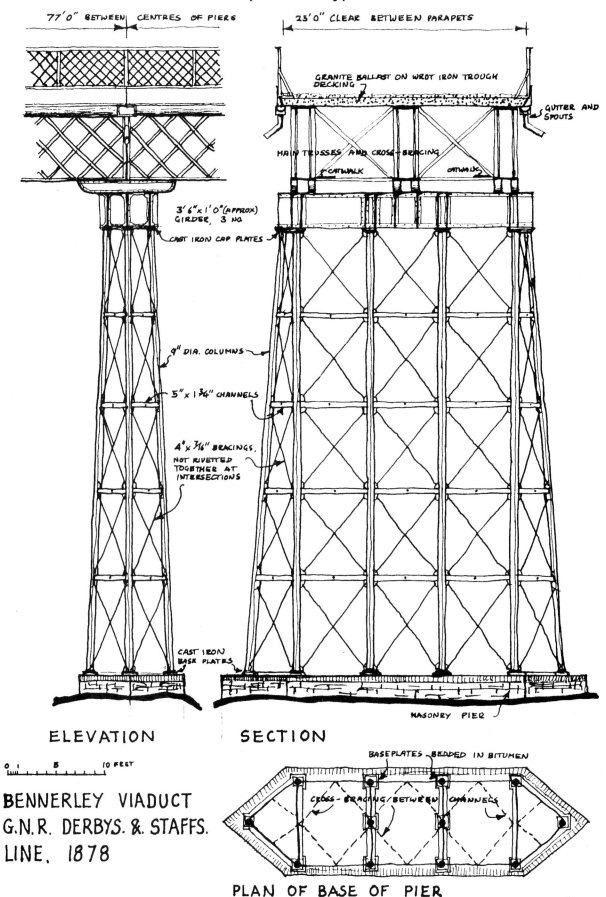

77'0" BETWEEN CENTRES OF PIERS

25'0" CLEAR BETWEEN PARAPETS

GRANITE BALLAST ON WROT IRON TROUGH DECKING

GUTTER AND SPOUTS

MAIN TRUSSES AND CROSS-BRACING

CATWALK

CATWALK

3'6" x 1'0" (APPROX) GIRDER, 3 No.

CAST IRON CAP PLATES

9" DIA. COLUMNS

5" x 1¾" CHANNELS

4" x ⁷⁄₁₆" BRACINGS. NOT RIVETTED TOGETHER AT INTERSECTIONS

CAST IRON BASE PLATES

MASONRY PIER

ELEVATION

SECTION

0 1 5 10 FEET

BENNERLEY VIADUCT
G.N.R. DERBYS. & STAFFS.
LINE, 1878

BASEPLATES BEDDED IN BITUMEN

CROSS-BRACING BETWEEN CHANNELS

PLAN OF BASE OF PIER

M.D.P.H. 2/72

146

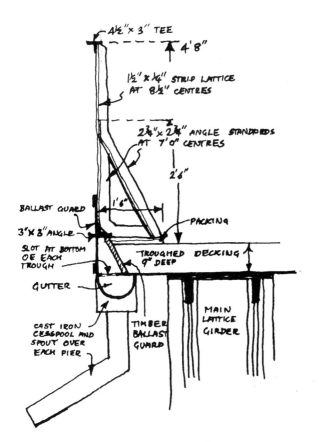

SECTION THRO' PARAPET

- 4½" × 3" TEE
- 4'8"
- 1½" × ¼" STRIP LATTICE AT 8½" CENTRES
- 2¾" × 2¾" ANGLE STANDARDS AT 7'0" CENTRES
- 2'6"
- 1'6"
- BALLAST GUARD
- PACKING
- 3" × 3" ANGLE
- SLOT AT BOTTOM OF EACH TROUGH
- TROUGHED DECKING 9" DEEP
- GUTTER
- MAIN LATTICE GIRDER
- CAST IRON CESSPOOL AND SPOUT OVER EACH PIER
- TIMBER BALLAST GUARD

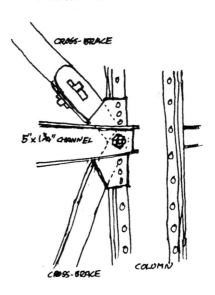

PLAN OF COLUMN

- RIVETS AT 6" CENTRES
- 2½"
- 9" DIA.
- ¾" WROT IRON
- 1" DIA. BOLT.
- ½" GUSSET PLATES
- ½" PACKINGS
- PINNED CONNECTION
- VERTICAL CROSS-BRACE

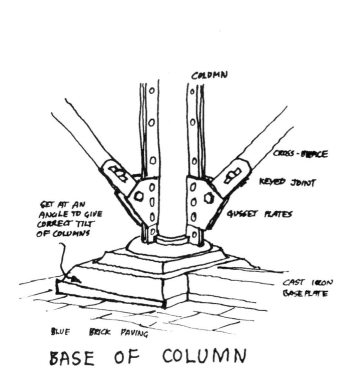

BASE OF COLUMN

- COLUMN
- CROSS-BRACE
- KEYED JOINT
- GUSSET PLATES
- SET AT AN ANGLE TO GIVE CORRECT TILT OF COLUMNS
- CAST IRON BASE PLATE
- BLUE BRICK PAVING

JUNCTION OF BRACING WITH COLUMN

- CROSS-BRACE
- 5" × 1¾" CHANNEL
- CROSS-BRACE
- COLUMN

BENNERLEY VIADUCT

M.D.P. HAMMOND   FEB. 1972

Appendix 4B
BENNERLEY (ILKESTON) VIADUCT

This viaduct was opened in January 1878 to carry the Great northern Railway's Derbyshire and Staffordshire line across the Erewash Valley, between Awsworth and Ilkeston. It was designed by Richard Johnson, at that time the railway company's Chief Civil Engineer. The whole structure is 1,440 feet long and up to 60 feet high, and is approached at each end by high embankments pierced by girder spans over the Erewash Canal to the west and the Nottingham Canal to the east .The structure is of wrought iron, with brick abutments. It consists of sixteen spans of 77 feet, each measured from the centre of each wrought iron lattice pier, and at the western end, three plate girder spans on brick piers over the main Erewash Valley railway lines from Trent Junction. Apart from these and two of the 16 spans which cross the River Erewash and the access road to a coal depot, the viaduct stands on a strip of waste ground about a hundred feet wide.

Each wrought iron pier consists of twelve vertical and slightly inclined columns of 9" diameter and up to 45 feet high. The lower ends rest on cast iron baseplates on a boat-shaped masonry foundation, and the upper ends are joined together by three 3' 6" x 1'0" transverse rolled sections, bolted to cast iron capping plates which take up the Inclination of the columns. The columns are braced together with horizontal 5" x 1¾" channels and 4" x ½" cross-bracing, with bolted or pinned connections. Each span is carried on three parallel lattice girders, each 7' 6" deep and 2' 6" wide, with horizontal and vertical cross-bracing between then. The horizontal bracing carries timber catwalks for maintenance purposes. The track is laid on ballast on 9" deep troughed decking. Slots at the ends of each trough drain into a half-round gutter about a foot wide, which runs along under the parapets. The parapets are 4' 8" high, measured from the top of the decking, and are made up of a diagonal lattice of 1½" x 1¼" strip at 8½" pitch, with a 4½" x 3" tee top member and a 3" x 3" angle bottom member, and supported at 7ft centres by standards of 2¾" x 2¾" angle, rivetted to the decking and braced.

The east abutment is mainly of red brick, with a few patches of repair worn in blue brick. Much of the short section of parapet to this, with its stone copings, has been pulled down. The bricks themselves are in good condition, but the mortar is a soft grey lime mortar, and much of the abutment needs repointing. The brickwork of the other piers and abutments is of blue brick in cement mortar, and is in good condition.

Although the structure has been out of use for some time the metalwork is generally in very good condition it was painted with black bituminous paint, and very little rust is showing anywhere. The worst affected parts are the track drainage gutters, which have rusted away completely in parts. The fact that they are practically inaccessible for cleaning will have contributed to this. They drain into a cast iron cistern head with a spout over each pier.

This viaduct is one of the few remaining examples of this type of construction, and certainly the only one left in the East Midlands area. It was probably designed thus because of poor subsoil conditions and local colliery workings, which would have affected a masonry structure adversely.

It seems that the bridges in the approach embankments are to be removed in the near future, and if the viaduct is to be retained, then access to it will be a problem. If it is to be used as a motor road, or even a cycle track and pedestrian walkway, then steps and long approach ramps will be needed, and I am sure the climb will deter many people from using it. There are certainly some good views from the top of the viaduct.

A portion of the viaduct could be preserved, either in a museum or in situ, with suitable access for reasonably close inspection by the public.

If it were really impossible to preserve any part of the viaduct, then the structure should be thoroughly recorded in detailed drawings and photographs by some competent persons.

M. D. P. Hammond
March 1972

Appendix 5
1936 Passenger Ticket and Wagon Statistics

	SINGLE	RETURN	WEEKLY	MONTHLY	3 MONTH	ANNUAL	PARCELS FORWD.	RECVD.	TICKETS COLLECTED
Awsworth	1125	9675	-	66	5	-	12	1101	9955
Basford	2504	70973	2568	206	157	6	3148	11121	112467
Codnor	1553	59622	3	730	54	4	92	4086	70500
Eastwood	869	21969	-	103	25	24	833	14644	37825
Heanor	-	777							
Ilkeston	2948	108959	215	224	88	4	10074	13824	176000
Kimberley	1864	68005	623	367	111	94	2982	7616	89486
Newthorpe	423	13657	-	70	4	17	449	286	16287
Pinxton	2578	66059	67	1869	6	18	1061	2999	85750
Pye Hill	2401	22662	8	756	1	10	4196	312	33600

WAGONS FORWARDED AND RECEIVED

	WAGONS FORWD.	RECVD.
Awsworth	206	58
Basford	4249	5327

	GOODS FORWD.	RECVD.	MINERALS FORWD.	RECVD.	COAL FORWD.	RECVD.
Codnor	2192	823	1168	1885	10190	13
Eastwood	843	2003	214	60	-	39
Heanor	32	577	4	36	-	20
Ilkeston	842	3676	215	290	-	788
Stanton (GN)	17416	1435	5168	40592	-	21000
Kimberley	474	1462	4156	145	-	112
Newthorpe	3	88	34	12	-	540
Pinxton	54	1137	229	154	15800	11
Pye Hill	67	217	-	-	-	-

The main colliery traffic was dealt with at the Mineral Agents/Accounts Office. Only a few stations dealt with their own such as Codnor and Pinxton.

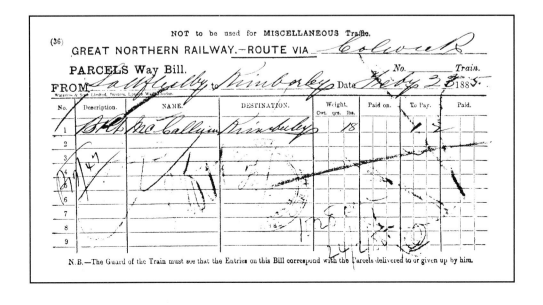

Appendix 6
Ilkeston Traffic Statement
October 1923 to 31st March 1924 (6 Months)

153,853   Tickets issued for   £6,841.00

894   Season Tickets for   £1,044.00

10,331   Parcels

27   Horses   } total receipts £446.00

512   Milk Churns

30,235 Wagons of coal forwarded excluding Stanton Branch

331,511 tons ironstone, pipes, slag received and forwarded   } Stanton

66,070 tons coal and coke received and forwarded   } Branch

200,000 wagons attached and detached in yards

43 Traffic staff   33 Permanent way   Wages £230 for 6 months

Appendix 7
Station Masters Responsibilities on 23rd November 1900

SIGNAL BOXES AND GROUND FRAMES

KIMBERLEY STATION MASTER - Nuthall Sidings Box, East Box (Open as required), West Box, Awsworth Junction.

NEWTHORPE STATION MASTER - Station Box, Digby Colliery.

EASTWOOD STATION MASTER - South Box, North Box, Pollington.

CODNOR PARK STATION MASTER - Brinsley Sidings, Brinsley Junction (Joint with MR), Station Box.

PYE HILL STATION MASTER - Station Box.

PINXTON STATION MASTER - Station Box, Palmerston Junction.

AWSWORTH STATION MASTER - Station Box.

ILKESTON STATION MASTER - East Box, West Box, Nutbrook Junction, Stanton Junction, Fork Junction.

Appendix 8

Operational Statistics
Kimberley & District, 1933-34

The stationmaster 'on call' at Kimberley was later responsible for all railway operations between Nuthall and West Hallam inclusive, a distance of 7 1/4 miles. These comprised:

- 2 Passenger and Goods stations (Kimberley and Awsworth).
- 1 Goods station (Kimberley Midland).
- 2 Public sidings Watnall (GN and Midland), GN siding was closed on 1st February 1954.
- 2 Private sidings (Hardy & Hanson's Breweries, Midland Railway).
- 1 Colliery (2 reception sidings, GN and Midland).
- 1 Sand quarry.
- 1 Junction.
- 7 1/2 miles of main line (half in each direction).
- 3 miles of single line (LMS).

Kimberley LNE Station
An average of 190 trains passed through every 24 hours (both directions) of which:

55 were stopping passenger trains (Monday to Friday)
69 were stopping passenger trains (Saturday)
12 were stopping passenger trains (Sunday)
and numerous excursion trains

The staff comprised:
- 3 signalmen grade 3
- 2 adult class 5 clerks   )
- 1 adult porter Grade 2   )   for passengers
- 2 lad porters   )

- 1 leading porter   ) for
- 1 carting agent   ) goods

The throughput was:

	No.	£			Tons
Booked Passengers:	159,658	3,176	Carted:		957
Season Tickets:	1,262	627	Not carted:		2,417
			(station to station)		
Parcels forwarded:	7,571	372	Minerals:		29,635
Parcels received:	7,520	----------	(excl. coal and coke)		
		£4,175			

Nuthall Sand Siding (Stanton Iron Co.):   Annual Output: 3,020 wagons,   25,000 tons

Nuthall Sidings: 3 signalmen, Grade 3

Watnall Branch (B W & Co)

New Watnall Colliery: Output (Nov 1933 - Oct 1934)*

			No.	Tons
	Coal	LNE	6,228	53,000 tons
		LMS	6,711	58,292 tons
	Bricks	LNE		5,000 tons
		LMS		5,268 tons

Awsworth Junction: Average 190 trains in 24 hours   3 signalmen, Grade 3
                                                            2 shunters, Grade 4

Awsworth Station: 16 stopping passenger trains daily (Mon - Fri)   )   1 signalman, Grade 5
                        25 stopping passenger trains (Saturday)   )

* Traffic for both LNER and MR was often routed via Beggarlee sidings at Eastwood instead of Watnall (P. 55).

Ilkeston Wd°

GREAT NORTHERN RAILWAY.

Circular No. 12,741a.

HEANOR BRANCH.

SINGLE LINE WORKING

BETWEEN

NUTBROOK COLLIERY JUNCTION and HEANOR.

This branch is worked under the instructions in Appendix III. of the General rules and regulations.

The train staff described below must be carried on the engine, and without this staff no train or engine must be allowed to travel on the line.

DESCRIPTION OF TRAIN STAFF.

Lettered on one side—   Lettered on the other side—

GO ON   GO ON
TO   TO
HEANOR.   NUTBROOK.

The train staff, which will be required to release the points at Heanor station, must, when not in use, be kept in the signal box at Nutbrook junction, and, on arrival there of any train for the Heanor branch, the fireman must obtain the train staff from the signalman. The signalman must not allow the train to enter upon the single line until he is satisfied the staff is in possession of the engineman on the engine.

When a train or engine from the branch has arrived at Nutbrook Colliery junction, and is clear of the single line, the fireman must hand the train staff to the signalman, who will go to the engine to receive it and will not allow the train to proceed towards Ilkeston until he has received the train staff.

Should a train or engine for the Heanor section arrive at Nutbrook Colliery junction when the train staff is not there, such train or engine must be detained till the staff arrives.

In working over the Heanor branch there must be a brake in front and one in rear of each train.

No engine or train must pass the Marlpool station without stopping there.

NUTBROOK COLLIERY.

The engine of the Colliery Company will take wagons between the colliery and the sidings at Nutbrook only. It must not at any time be upon or foul of the Railway Company's running line, nor must it be upon or foul of the sidings when the Railway Company's engine is there or due to be there.

Cancels 12750A   17.08 1898.

J. ALEXANDER,
Superintendent of the line.

Appendix 10
Circulars 5720, 6036 I & R Morleys Nottingham, Heanor

LONDON AND NORTH EASTERN RAILWAY.

District Superintendent's Office,
Victoria Station,
NOTTINGHAM : 18th November, 1932.

CIRCULAR 5720.

PASSENGER TRAIN SERVICE BETWEEN NOTTINGHAM AND HEANOR
FOR THE CONVEYANCE OF MESSRS. I.&.R. MORLEYS' WORK PEOPLE.

Commencing on Monday, 21st November, additional passenger trains will run as under:-

      8.12 a.m. Ilkeston to Heanor.
      5.45 p.m. Heanor to Nottingham (S)
      12.15 p.m. Heanor to Nottingham (SO).

Details of the working are as under:-

OUTWARD.

Two thirds and one third brake to be attached each week-day to rear of 7. 3 a.m. Basford & Bulwell to Derby (via Gedling) and detached at Ilkeston, forming an additional passenger train as under:-

		a.m.
Ilkeston.	dep.	8.12.
Stanton Junction.	"	8A13.
Nutbrook Junction.	"	8B15.
Heanor.	arr.	8.21.

Tickets to be collected at Ilkeston.

GUARD:-   No.80 Working.

ENGINE:-   Off 7. 2 a.m. Nottingham to Ilkeston.

Engine and Guard to return light to Ilkeston as under and take up booked working:-

		a.m.
Heanor.	dep.	8.30.
Ilkeston.	arr.	8.39.

RETURN.

Light engine, with Guard, to run each week-day as under:-

		(S) p.m.	(S.O) a.m.
Nutbrook Junction	dep.	5.20.	11.50.
Heanor.	arr.	5.30.	12. 0.

Additional passenger train, Heanor to Nottingham, to run each week-day as under:-

		(S) p.m.	(S.O) p.m.
Heanor.	dep.	5.45.	12.15.
Nutbrook Junction	"	5A51.	12A21.
Ilkeston.	"	5B54.	12B24.
Awsworth Junction.	pass	5.59.	12.29.
Bagthorpe Junction.	"	6. 6.	12.36.
New Basford.	dep.	6. 8.	12.38.
Nottingham (Vic)	arr.	6.13.	12.43.

GUARD:-   No.100 Working (S), and 152 Working (SO).

Engine:-   Nutbrook pilot 100 Working (S), off 9.30. a.m. Heanor.

LONDON AND NORTH EASTERN RAILWAY.
District Superintendent's Office,
Victoria Station,
NOTTINGHAM . 16th January 1935.

Circular No. 6036.

PASSENGER TRAIN SERVICE BETWEEN NOTTINGHAM AND
HEANOR FOR THE CONVEYANCE OF MESSRS I. & R.
MORLEY'S WORKPEOPLE.

With reference to my Circular No. 5720 dated 18th November 1932.

The second paragraph on Page 4 of the Circular should be amended to read as under :-

"In connection with the working of these additional passenger trains, Crossing Keepers must be in charge at Meynell's Crossing, Shipley Colliery Company's Brick Yard Coppice Crossing and the Heanor Coppice Level Crossing and the gates kept open for the passing of the trains. In the case of the gates at Heanor Coppice Crossing, these will be attended to by the Heanor Porter, and those at Meynell's Coppice Crossing and the Shipley Colliery Company's Brick Yard Coppice Crossing by the Engineer's staff. The gates must be open in sufficient time to prevent delay to the trains."

Please advise all concerned.

E.W.ROSTERN.
District Superintendent.

The Great Northern Railway 1576

District Superintendents Office,

Nottingham Station.

Please refer hereto.

DL277   Aug 6th 18.6

    10626

      Dear sir

          Colliery engines using Ilkeston Turn-Tables
          - - - - - - - - - - - - - - -

          Please note that whenever the West Hallam, Manners,
or Ilkeston Colliery Companies require to use our Turn Table
for turning their engines a charge of 2/6 is to be made for the
use of the lines approaching thereto and the use of the Turn-
Table.   The Charge of 2/6 is per engine.   Ack: receipt.
      Chief Goods Managers D35/219
                  47417

      Mr Alexander's 83649. 1896.

                    yours truly

MR Barratt

    Ilkeston.

(P 9—25 bks., 200 lvs.—5-19.)   No. 3590

G.N.R. Loco. Dept. Colwick, 24/9/ 19 20

To the Station Master at _Nutbrook_

  Please allow driver _G Bown_

Engine No. _126_ to obtain a supply of coal from
wagon No. _Stage_ at your station.

                C. H. LAVERICK,

_40_ cwts obtained.   per

                    W Clarke Station Master.

W. & S. Ltd.]

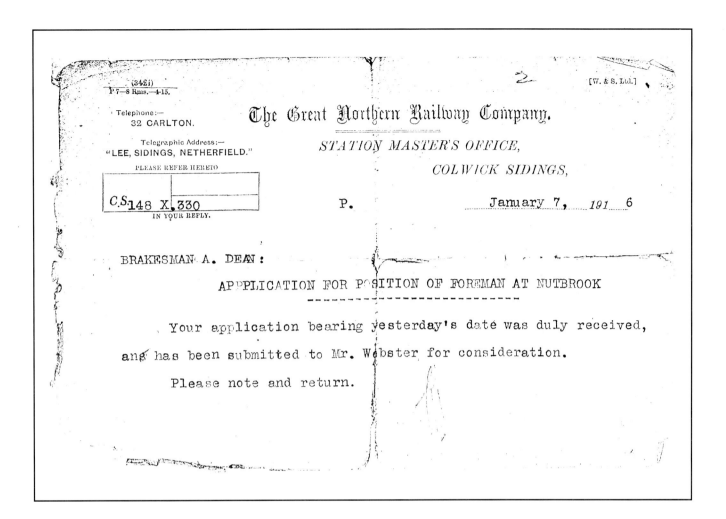

(342i)
P 7—8 Rms.—4-15.

Telephone:—
32 CARLTON.

Telegraphic Address:—
"LEE, SIDINGS, NETHERFIELD."

PLEASE REFER HERETO

[W. & S. Ltd.]

The Great Northern Railway Company.

STATION MASTER'S OFFICE,

COLWICK SIDINGS,

C.S. 148 X. 330

IN YOUR REPLY.

P.   January 7,   191 6

BRAKESMAN A. DEAN:

APPPLICATION FOR POSITION OF FOREMAN AT NUTBROOK

Your application bearing yesterday's date was duly received,
and has been submitted to Mr. Webster for consideration.

Please note and return.

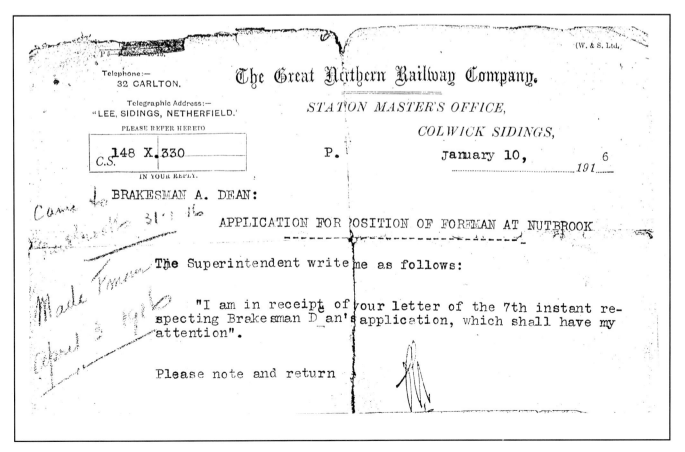

Telephone:—
32 CARLTON.

Telegraphic Address:—
"LEE, SIDINGS, NETHERFIELD.'

PLEASE REFER HERETO

(W. & S. Ltd.)

The Great Northern Railway Company.

STATION MASTER'S OFFICE,

COLWICK SIDINGS,

C.S. 148 X. 330

IN YOUR REPLY.

P.   January 10,   6
                                                191

BRAKESMAN A. DEAN:

APPLICATION FOR POSITION OF FOREMAN AT NUTBROOK

The Superintendent write me as follows:

"I am in receipt of your letter of the 7th instant re-
specting Brakesman Dean's application, which shall have my
attention".

Please note and return

SOME OTHER RCTS BOOKS

THE GREAT NORTHERN RAILWAY IN THE EAST MIDLANDS
Nottingham Victoria and the GC Line, The Leen Valley Network and Extensions

As the GNR built Northwards from Nottingham, the Manchester, Sheffield and Lincolnshire (later Great Central) Railway built South from Sheffield. The two companies agreed to jointly build a major twelve platform station in the heart of Nottingham, nearer to the centre than any other station, and opened it on the queen's birthday in 1900 as Nottingham Victoria. Had the station lasted longer it would surely have been preserved, with its tall, elegant clock tower leading into fine platform level architecture under the imposing roof. . In the Leen Valley a plethora of competing lines were provided to serve the extensive collieries and ironworks. Author Alf Henshaw brings vividly to life the smoky air of Victoria station and the complexity of the North Notts railway scene with his extensive atmospheric photographs. *Size 212 x 272mm, laminated cover, 108 pages, 262 photos*

THE GREAT NORTHERN RAILWAY IN THE EAST MIDLANDS
The Rise and Fall of Colwick Yards, Nottingham London Rd-Gedling-Basford

Today its hard to imagine the North Nottinghamshire towns of Basford, Bulwell and Gedling handling express and local passenger trains, and major mineral flows serving the iron ore, coal and steel industries. The GNR built their main line from the Trent climbing across to the Leen Valley and developed the railway town of Netherfield. Their Colwick yards complex was vast, with capacity for 6,000 wagons and employing 600. Multiple signalboxes and two engine sheds, one with eight roads, were features, as were the substantial stations. The complete story of construction, expansion, intensive operation, contraction, closure and the scene today is presented by retired railwayman and new local author Alfred Henshaw. Extensive maps and signal diagrams are featured. *Large page size 212 x 272mm, laminated cover, 108 pages, 262 illustrations through maps, signal diagrams and photographs*

THE BIRKENHEAD RAILWAY
(LMS & GW Joint)

Today's successful electric railway between Chester and Birkenhead is in sharp contrast to the earlier story of the line. At first passengers were the major earner, but opening of other lines at Chester and the development of Ellesmere Port brought major freight operations. The main line was quadrupled, and the dock system eventually grew to 48 miles. Author Bruce Maund brings to life the detailed and fascinating tale of the complete system, the machinations of expanding railway companies to get control and, in the end, an object lesson in how two great rivals found a satisfactory *modus operandi* to run it with reasonable harmony for almost 90 years. Compulsory reading for all those involved in today's fragmented railways! *Page size 277 x 212mm, laminated cover, 136 pages, 140 illustrations.*

GREAT NORTHERN LOCOMOTIVE HISTORY

This major four volume work covers the complete story of the Great Northern Railway, Doncaster Works and its locomotives, from earliest days to The Grouping. Each class is covered from all six designers - Cubitt, Bury, Sturrock, Stirling, Ivatt and Gresley. 1,553 Doncaster built engines are covered, plus those bought in. Their robust design was demonstrated by almost half of the GN stock passed to the LNER at Grouping surviving into British Railways ownership 25 years later.
The set totals 804 pages with 738 illustrations. Buy the complete set or individual volumes.

BRITISH RAILWAYS STANDARD STEAM LOCOMOTIVES
Volume 1 Background to Standardisation and the Pacific Classes

Immediately British Railways was formed in January 1948, the railway Executive instructed Robert Riddles to design a series of standard locomotive designs. The intention was to gain material savings in running and maintenance costs by adopting as standard the best practices of the four independent companies. In this major new series, the Society presents for the first time the complete story of British locomotive standardisation from the days of the Robinson ROD 2-8-0s to the twelve BR Standard designs totalling 999 locomotives. This book, by Paul Chancellor and Peter Gilbert , presents the Standards design history and for each of the 66 locomotives in the popular Britannia, Duke and Clan classes its complete construction, modification, allocation and operating history. *Page size 212 x 272mm, Casebound, 184 pages, 151 illustrations including 17 in colour*

BRITISH RAILWAYS STANDARD STEAM LOCOMOTIVES
Volume 3 The Tank Engine Classes

From Penzance to Wick, the Standard tank classes were designed to modernise secondary route power. Railway enthusiasts throughout the land became familiar with their high running plates which gave the 230 engines of three types their "family" appearance. Author Paul Chancellor presents their full story, from their design origins, construction, modifications, allocation, use and liveries. Whether these engines hauled you reluctantly to school - your reviewer's experience - or you only came across them in preservation, the Class 4's handsome curved tank sides will evoke many a nostalgic memory. With their construction at all six main workshops, local livery variations and national use, there is something for everyone to savour in this book, the second in the Society's BR Standard series. Diagrams of each design are included. *Page size 212 x 272mm, Casebound, 189 photographs including sixteen in colour.*

A TRAVELLERS GUIDE TO THE ROBIN HOOD LINE

A Travellers Guide to the Robin Hood Line presents an illustrated history of the line and its rebuilding as a traveller can now view it heading north from Nottingham to Worksop. Full colour covers, art paper production. Each section of the route is dealt with in detail, using a one page map/one page narrative layout covering not only railway but also local history and topographical features. Our thanks go to the East Midlands Branch for their efforts, especially John Hitchens and Frank Ashley, and we thank Nottinghamshire County Council for sponsoring much of its production cost to allow an extremely competitive price.
A5 size, laminated cover, 28 pages, 25 illustrations including three in colour and ten maps

RAISING STEAM ON THE LMS
The Evolution of LMS Locomotive Boilers

This absorbing read opens at Grouping with an LMS locomotive fleet of poor steaming designs unsuited to the heavy and growing traffic levels. The Board's historic decision to hire Stanier from the rival Great Western and his revolutionary work to equip the LMS with a more suitable locomotive fleet revolved around more effective raising and use of steam. The complete story is presented here, from early LMS practice based on pre-Grouping designs, through Stanier's importation of GWR practices, early results and comprehensive details of his design improvements culminating in the largest British pacifics, the Coronation class. The necessary technical content is presented by author Arthur Cook coincisely in useful tables and an Appendix, allowing the text to be presented in an infectious, readable style. Readers can almost imagine themselves in the mutual improvement classes at the running shed!
Casebound, page size 180 x 235mm, 233 pages, 138 photographs and drawings, including one in colour

RCTS Publications List

*UK Post Free
Overseas add 25%

Title of Book	ISBN No	*Price
The Great Northern Railway in the East Midlands		
The Erewash Valley lines, Pinxton Branch,		
Awsworth-Ilkeston, Heanor & Stanton Branches	0901115886	**£15-95**
Nottingham Vic,GC,Leen Valley Network	090111586X	**£14-95**
Colwick Yards,London Rd-Gedling-Basford	0901115843	**£13-95**
The Birkenhead Railway	0901115878	**£14-95**
Special Offer Set of Gt Northern Loco History		**£40-95**
1: 1847-1866	0901115614	**£12-95**
2: 1867-1895	0901115746	**£19-95**
3A: 1896-1911	090111569X	**£19-95**
3B: 1911-1923	0901115703	**£16-95**
BR Standard Steam Locomotives:		
Vol 1 Background and the Pacifics	0901115819	**£19-95**
Vol 3 The Tank Engine Classes	0901115770	**£19-95**
A Travellers Guide to the Robin Hood line	0901115835	**£ 2-95**
The High Level Bridge and Newcastle Central Station	1873513283	£ 9-95
Locomotives of the LNER:		
Part 1 Preliminary Survey	0901115118	£12-95
Part 2A Tender Engines A1-A10	0901115258	£14-95
Part 2B Tender Engines Classes B1-B19	0901115738	£13-95
Part 9A Tank Engines Classes L1-L19	0901115401	£10-95
Part 9B Tank Engines Classes Q1-Z5	090111541X	£10-95
Part 10A Departmental Stock, Engine Sheds,		
Boiler and Tender Numbering	0901115657	£10-95
Locomotives of the LMS:		
Raising Steam on the LMS	0901115851	£24-95
LMS Diesels	0901115762	£19-95
LMS Locomotive Names	0901115797	£18-95
Highland Railway Locomotives 1855-1895	0901115649	£12-95
Highland Railway Locomotives 1895-1923	090111572X	£16-95
The Railways of Keynsham	0901115827	£16-95
Western Change-Summer Saturdays in the West	0901115789	£15-95

Available from:-

*Hon Assistant Publications Officer
Hazelhurst
Tiverton Road
Bampton
Devon EX16 9LJ*

When ordering please quote reference GNEM3